THE MANDALA BOOK

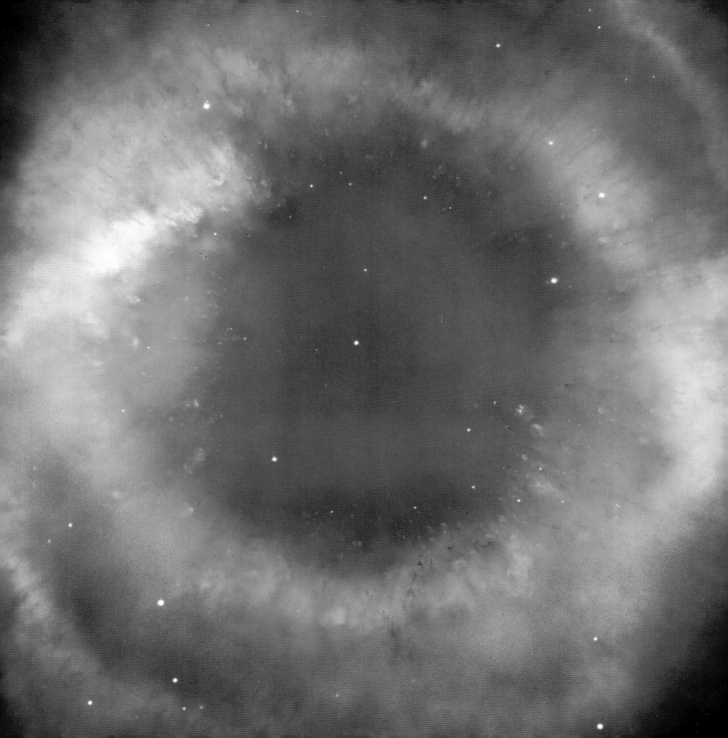

THE MANDALA BOOK
PATTERNS OF THE UNIVERSE

LORI BAILEY CUNNINGHAM

STERLING
New York

STERLING and the distinctive Sterling logo are registered trademarks of
Sterling Publishing Co., Inc.

Library of Congress Cataloging-in-Publication Data
Cunningham, Lori Bailey.
 The mandala book : patterns of the universe / Lori Bailey Cunningham.
  p. cm.
 Includes bibliographical references and index.
 ISBN 978-1-4027-6290-1
 1. Tantras. I. Title.
 BL604.M36C87 2010
 203'.7--dc22
                                                              2010013347

8 10 9

Published by Sterling Publishing Co., Inc.
1166 Avenue of the Americas, New York, NY 10036
© 2010 by Lori Bailey Cunningham
Distributed in Canada by Sterling Publishing
c/o Canadian Manda Group, 664 Annette Street
Toronto, Ontario, Canada M6S 2C8
Distributed in the United Kingdom by GMC Distribution Services
Castle Place, 166 High Street, Lewes, East Sussex, England BN7 1XU
Distributed in Australia by Capricorn Link (Australia) Pty. Ltd.
P.O. Box 704, Windsor, NSW 2756, Australia
Please see picture credits on page 308 for copyright information

Design concept: Lori Bailey Cunningham
Design: Gavin Motnyk

Printed in China
All rights reserved

ISBN 978-1-4027-6290-1

For information about custom editions, special sales, premium and
corporate purchases, please contact Sterling Special Sales
Department at 800-805-5489 or specialsales@sterlingpublishing.com.

Frontispiece: A composite picture of the Helix Nebula, assembled by the Space Telescope Science
Institute in Baltimore from images taken by the NASA Hubble Space Telescope and the National
Science Foundation's telescope at Kitt Peak National Observatory near Tucson, Arizona.

To Mom and Dad, Rien, Devan, Gavon, and David, my partner on the path.

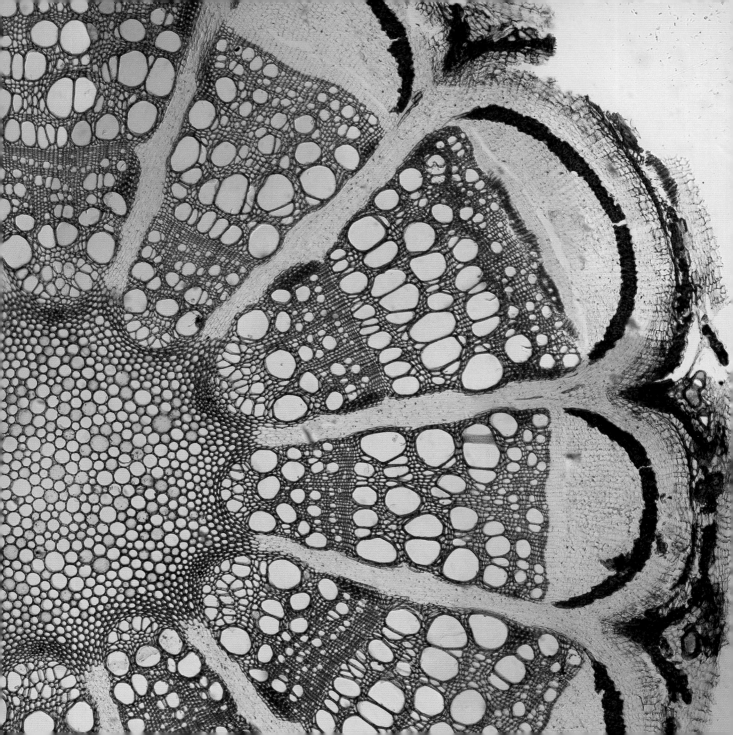

CONTENTS

Opposite: Microphotograph of a
Clematis root cross section.

SEEING WITH NEW EYES

The real voyage of discovery consists not in seeking new lands,
but in seeing with new eyes.

MARCEL PROUST

This book is about me and you and everything in between. It's about what we're made of, what we experience, and it hints at things that defy our imagination. It's also about shapes and how they describe a very important part of what we are: connected elements evolving from, and revolving around a unifying center—the mandala. Recognition of patterns and shapes can profoundly affect how we see ourselves in relation to each other and the world in which we live, to embrace ideas that unite us, not divide us. In observing connections, we can establish associations that lead to kinship and the possibility of peace.

What if we could recapture, again and again, that exquisite amazement we experience when seeing something for the first time? What if there was a key to unlock that precious place in which childlike curiosity is stored? Would we take it? Would we use it? Those who have considered these questions offer this key: Look with new eyes.

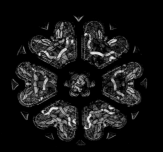

Left: Circular stained glass window, location unknown.

Opposite: Passionflower.

Order is the shape
upon which beauty
depends.

Pearl S. Buck

BEGINNING THE JOURNEY

To begin this journey, we first need to learn about the mandala. It is the concept around which this book is structured and is related to everything you'll be seeing and reading about. To become aware of the mandala is to become conscious of what is going on around us, and it is this consciousness that helps us see our connection to the world and to one another.

The pattern found within the mandala can help describe the nature of our being as well as the nature of our cosmos. The study of mandalas often includes contemplating the core of reality, what is at the "true center" of the world in which we live.

Above left to right: The mouth of a jellyfish is located in the animal's center and is surrounded by a circular umbrella, composed mostly of a gelatinous material; Celestial objects display circular patterns in their visual appearance as well as in their spinning and rotational movements.

Opposite: Purple morning glory with bug.

You are the center
of your own and in
the periphery of the
kyil-khors [mandalas]
of others.

Ngakpa Chögyam &
Khandro Déchen

Most of us already hold ideas, to one degree or another, about how the world came into being and is structured. Some of our beliefs are commonly shared; some might seem to conflict with beliefs held by others. Yet the mandala can serve as a structure within which a variety of ideas and beliefs can be viewed and shared. Students of the mandala are attracted to its ability to transcend "either/or" in favor of "and." The mandala connects, rather than divides, us.

Above: Eight legs of a spider extend from the hub of its body.

Opposite: Macro shot of a poppy flower.

Mathematics is not only
a thread by which we
may know the Beyond
but also a means
by which we may
commune with it.

Thomas J. McFarlane

WHAT IS A MANDALA?

The term used for the circular pattern that describes the images and concepts in this book is *mandala*, an ancient Sanskrit word which, literally defined, means "circle." Both words—*mandala* and *circle*—are used interchangeably throughout the book to describe qualities of each geometric shape that is discussed.

Another description of a mandala is used by Tibetan Buddhists, as described by Kennard Lipman and Merrill Peterson in their translation of Longchenpa's book, *You Are the Eyes of the World* (1987). It will also serve as our guide in this book: "An integrated structure organized around a unifying center."

That's saying a lot!

The mandala pattern is expressed artistically in many religious and philosophical traditions.

Clockwise from top left: Painted 19th-century Tibetan mandala of the Naropa tradition, Rubin Museum of Art, New York; Painted yin-yang decoration, origin unknown; Star of David engraved in stone, origin unknown.

Opposite: *The Four Seasons* by Saint Hildegard of Bingen (1098–1179), from *De operatione dei* (Works of God). Rupertsburg, Germany, ca. 1163–73 CE, Biblioteca Statale, Lucca, Italy.

TIBETAN MANDALAS

In the Tibetan Buddhist tradition, the mandala (*kyil khor* in Tibetan) is used to assist in meditation and is considered to be a diagram of the cosmos, a "blueprint for buddhahood." As Denise Patry Leidy describes them in her book *Mandala: The Architecture of Enlightenment* (1997), co-written with Robert Thurman, mandalas are "sacred places which, by their very presence in the world, remind a viewer of the immanence of sanctity in the universe and its potential in himself."

A mandala can also describe a situation in which learning takes place. Longchenpa states in his book, *You Are the Eyes of the World* (1987), "The five excellencies are the teacher, the message, the audience, the site, and the time. All five define spiritual communication. When whatever is experienced appears as these five excellencies, this situation is known as a mandala."

Mandalas are also tools for spiritual meditations. In Tibetan mandalas, each element has a special symbolic meaning that the meditator must consider. Meditating on a mandala is not a dreamy occupation; it is a focused activity in which the practitioner imagines the entire world of being through the lens of the mandala—not to escape reality, but to see it for what it truly is. This type of meditation also promotes the experience of boundless compassion for others as well as oneself by recognizing the truth of unity of all things.

Tibetan mandalas are constructed in a variety of forms, two- and three-dimensional, as well as in visualizations during meditation. A sand mandala is a two-dimensional *kyil khor* and is a collaborative creation meticulously constructed by a group of monks often over a period of one to several weeks. After carefully measuring and drawing out the mandala pattern, monks use instruments such as metal funnels to apply colored sand to the design (**top right**). After the mandala is completed (**opposite**), it is carefully dismantled in a ceremonial ritual that demonstrates the impermanence of life (**center right**). The sand is collected and dispersed into a nearby body of water as a blessing. **Bottom right**: Tibetan prayer flag pole. *Lung ta* prayer flags (meaning "Wind Horse" in Tibetan) are hung in high places, allowing the wind to carry the blessings depicted on the flags to all beings.

A mandala is also any circle, such as the disc of the sun or moon, and, by extension, any environment or surrounding, the sphere of influence of a kingdom, the circle of acquaintances of a person, and so forth.

Robert Thurman

If we consider the description of a mandala as applying to an atom, a structure organized around a nucleus, then it might mean that anything, even when not appearing circular in itself, is comprised of one or more—even an incalculable number of—mandalas. As José and Miriam Argüelles point out in their book, *Mandala* (1995), "The Mandala is earth and man, both the atom that composes the material essence of man and the galaxy of which the earth is but an atom."

The pattern of the mandala, "an integrated structure organized around a unifying center," is itself a sort of storybook describing aspects of the world in which we live. From the exquisitely simple to the powerfully complex concepts and structures we see in our world, mandalas represent diversity within unity—a gathering of many integrated into one.

The mandala can be seen as an entity that develops from "no-thing": The first manifested form of the primal point, a circle, evolves into a creative expression of a vast array of shapes, creating a pattern we see reflected throughout the physical universe. At every scale, from micro to macro, this pattern is repeated. The spherical orbs we observe in the sky and on which we live are composed of elements held together by the gravitational pull of a central core. From the electrons buzzing around the nuclei of atoms that create material forms, to planets orbiting around a sun, we see mandalas coming and going—all connected in an interwoven lattice of intricate beauty and complexity.

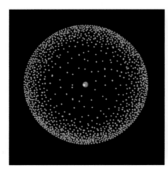 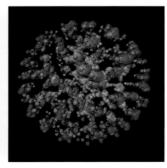

Left to right: Computer-generated image of a helium atom; Computer-generated image of the nucleus of a uranium atom.

Opposite: The Whirlpool Galaxy (Spiral Galaxy M51) is a classic spiral galaxy located in the Canes Venatici constellation.

The self, I thought, was like the monad which I am, and which is my world. The mandala represents this monad, and corresponds to the microcosmic nature of the psyche.

Carl Jung

Your body can be seen as a mandala. From the moment of conception, we evolve into increasingly complex life forms. Beginning with the tiny egg mandala from which you grew, cells—composed of molecules, composed of atoms that each contain a central nucleus—divide to create the uncountable elements that make up your body. Likewise, each of these individual parts, integrated structures within themselves, comes together to make the whole of a human body.

Your life is also a mandala. In each year, you complete a cycle, a mandala, with you at its center and around which revolves that year's events and experiences. Elongating that cycle, we see the mandala that is your life, which includes all events from birth through life and death.

You share your life with mandalas. Not only are you a mandala, but also, as you will see, innumerable things with which you come in contact are, in one way or another, mandalas comprised of even more mandalas. As Chögyam Trungpa describes the mandala principle in his book *Dharma Art* (1996), "It is that everything is related to everything else."

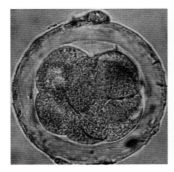 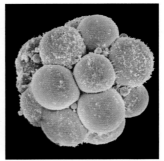

Left to right: Fertilized human egg, or zygote. When an egg has been fertilized, the resulting zygote begins to grow by dividing; Colored scanning electron micrograph image of a human embryo, or blastula, at the sixteen-cell stage, four days after fertilization. The blastula (from Greek *blastos*, meaning "sprout") is an early stage of embryonic development in animals.

Opposite: Human embryo at six to seven weeks.

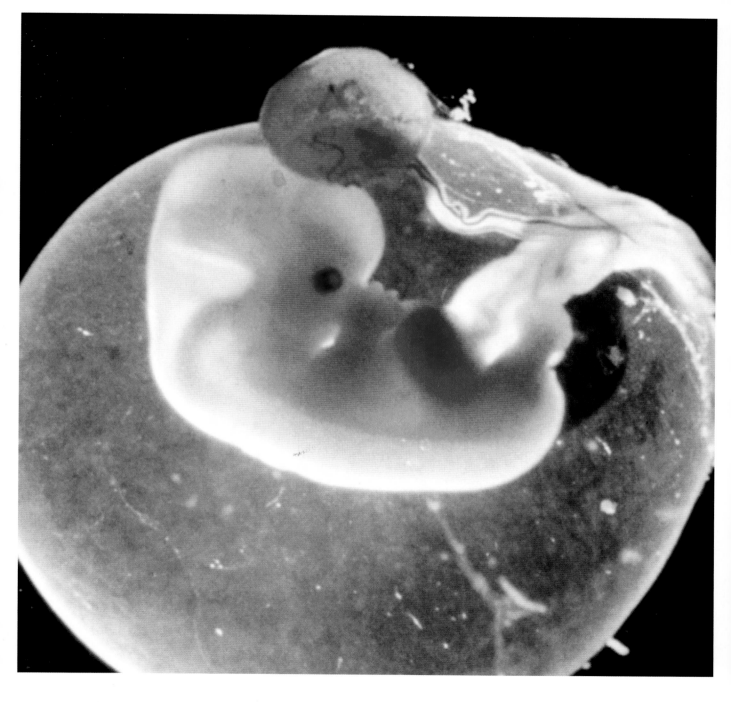

THE MANDALA PATTERN IN HUMAN CULTURE

We humans move in circles, and we participate in circles of community and relationships. These circles reflect, inform, and describe our physiological and psychological natures and the environmental nature of which we are a part. We cannot escape circles, nor would we want to.

In addition to the many examples of mandalas in nature, throughout this book you'll see a variety of mandalas as they appear in human culture, both as art forms and as objects. Some structures are created intentionally as mandalas, while others simply reflect mandalic traits, either in shape or concept. A mandala can be sacred, as when used in a spiritual ceremony or practice, or it can describe the basic structure or design of a substance or entity.

Understanding the primordial symbolism of the Mandala can lead not only to greater awareness, but ultimately to a transformation of the very ways in which man responds to the world in all its impulses.

José and Miriam Argüelles

Left: A general view of the festivities in Beijing National Stadium during the Closing Ceremony on August 24, 2008, for the Beijing 2008 Olympic Games.

Bottom left: A Whirling Dervish worshipping in an unknown location. Whirling Dervishes belong to the Mawlawi Order, a branch of Sufiism founded by the followers of Jalal ad-Din Muhammad Balkhi Rumi, a 13th-century Persian poet, Islamic jurist, and theologian.

Opposite—clockwise from top left: Native American dream catcher; Castlerigg stone circle near Keswick, England; Sunbeam streaming through the oculus in the Pantheon in Rome, Italy; *Raising the Dove* peace mandala during the Peace Alliance conference in Vancouver, Washington, 2008.

If we look closely at a flower, and likewise at other natural and man-made creations, we find a unity and an order common to all of them. This order can be seen in certain proportions which appear again and again, and also in the similarly dynamic way all things grow or are made—by a union of complementary opposites.

György Doczi

As a graphic element, the circle—a pattern that emanates from a center—can be used as a design motif in wallpaper, a company logo, or an abstract painting. Buildings have been erected based on mandalic patterns—some for spiritual reasons, others simply because designs based on a central geometric theme convey harmony and balance. As tools, mandalas are used to keep time, as with clocks and sundials. And in charts and diagrams, they provide a structure with which to organize information.

Powerfully conveying the idea of wholeness and unity, the circle is a symbol employed in many religious traditions. It has been used for thousands of years as a pattern to illustrate spiritual ideals and concepts. Mandalas continue to be used in healing and ceremonial rituals as well as in art forms to represent spiritual concepts.

Above: Stupa domes at sunset at the Shwedagon Pagoda (also known as the Golden Pagoda) in Yangon, Myanmar (Burma).

Bottom from left to right: Yin-yang horse logo by Maggie Macnab; Antique clock decorated with a painting of the sun; Chinese zodiac, or astrological calendar.

Opposite: Sundial constructed out of sand, rocks, and a feather.

Carl Gustav Jung, 1875–1961.

When I began drawing
the mandalas, however,
I saw that everything,
all the paths I had
been following, all
the steps I had taken,
were leading back to a
single point—namely, to
the mid-point. It became
increasingly plain to me
that the mandala is the
center. It is the exponent
of all paths. It is the
path to the center, to
individuation.

Carl Jung

Since the mandala requires no adherence to a specific belief system, nor does it necessarily imply a set of beliefs when used in conversation or creative activities, it is a tool that can be used comfortably in a variety of settings.

In the early twentieth century, Swiss psychoanalyst Carl Jung observed that mandala-making was used by many cultures in rituals to represent wholeness and healing. He saw the mandala as an archetypal pattern that symbolized the psyche's urge to find or experience wholeness (see page 226 in Chapter 7, "Patterns"). In his book *Man and His Symbols* (1968), Jung drew attention to the process of mandala-making as a way to facilitate healing through creating art, to "restore a previously existing order" as well as to give "expression and form to something that does not yet exist."

Meditation can be seen as a process of centering a mandalic activity that might even involve using mandalas as visual aids. Once considered solely a spiritual practice, counselors and psychologists have made meditation increasingly popular as a tool for relaxation and contemplation.

Left: *Rangoli* flower with *diyas* (traditional Indian lamps). Rangoli, a form of sand painting using finely ground powders, is one of the most popular art forms in India and is common during the Hindu festival of Diwali.

Opposite: Detail of *Quintessence: Life Itself*, by P. C. Turczyn, 2009.

Cognizance of
harmony in nature and
mathematics attunes us
to harmony at our
own core.

Michael Schneider

The mandala's transformative quality of wholeness blossoms when used for spiritual or personal growth. Whether they are used as an approach to quiet the mind or as an expression of spiritual ideals, mandalas provide a centered structure from which to explore and order our lives.

THE STARTING POINT

From a point, the pattern of the mandala radiates outward. The design that radiates outward from the center of the mandala is the reflection of what lies at the center; the ineffable center and its manifestation are integrated. The mandala is the entire expression—its center and all that radiates from the center. While a mandala may initially appear as a circle, it can morph into other shapes, as we will see. This does not mean that the essence of the mandala is lost, but simply that the outward expression of the mandala has changed—just as you look different now than you looked when you were two.

Left: Leaf resting on a stone
in a Zen garden.

Opposite: Vitarka mudra, a gesture of
discussion and transmission of Buddhist
teaching. Mudras are often used in yoga
meditation practice.

Mathematics thus
constitutes a thread to
the Beyond that has
never been lost.

Franklin Merrell-Wolff

This book utilizes geometry and pattern to examine the ways in which the mandala is manifested in our world. Geometry is the study of shapes. Pattern describes the predictable way things and events relate to each other. Together, geometry and pattern help to tell the story of how the mandala is expressed in the cosmos and in relationships.

The study of geometry can take you to some pretty interesting places where the mandala principle of wholeness is revealed in fascinating ways.

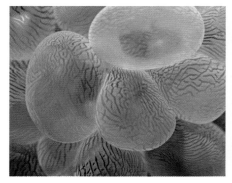

Clockwise from top left: Grape coral, also known as bubble coral; Turkey Tail mushroom growing on a log; Octopus.

Opposite: Seed pod of a lotus flower.

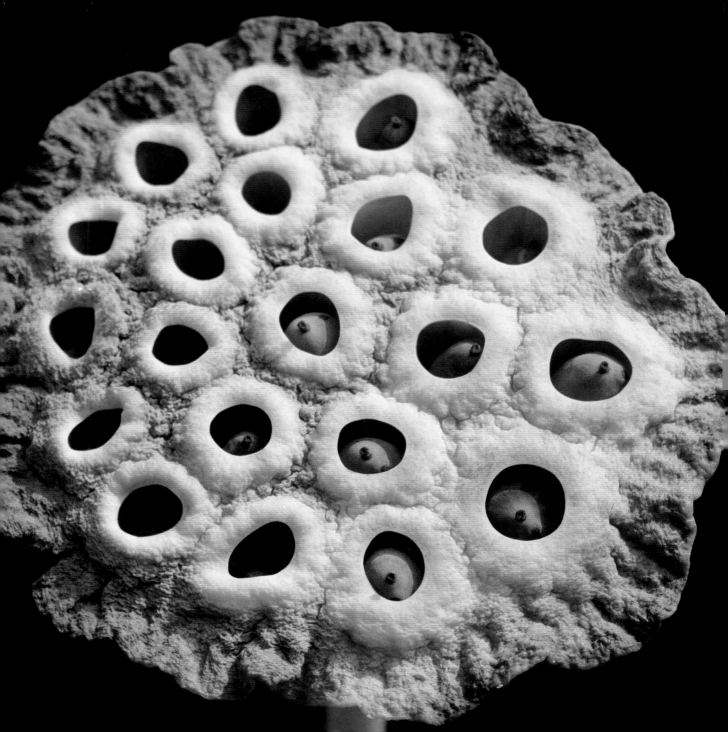

The universe may be
a mystery, but it's not
a secret.

Michael Schneider

In the first chapter, "Zero," we begin with a history of the same point that's at the center of the mandala. From there, geometry tells the story of how shapes take shape. The zero-dimensional point enters the first-dimensional community through the addition of another point to create a line. By adding a third point to the mix, you get two dimensions. Things get deep, so to speak, when four points come together, creating three dimensions. After a "Tour de Shapes," you'll enter the realm of patterns, which will enhance your appreciation of the shapes you just visited.

POINTS IN COMMON

It would seem that structured or ordered things do not exist without a center, a point around which they are organized. Material form is composed of particles that appear to revolve around a nucleus. Conversations go nowhere without a point and, indeed, without a point our own lives might seem meaningless.

But can we find the exact point, the exact center, of anything? Physics shows us that when observing the tiniest particles at highest magnification, we find space filled only with the potential for the existence of things. We can talk about these centers, yet we are unable to actually point to them.

Left—top row: Radial, hexagon, spiral;
center row: Triangle, circle, square;
bottom row: Dyad, pentagon, concentric.

Opposite—top row: Globe thistle, detail
of empty hornet nest, unfurling fern tip;
center row: Emerald swallowtail butterfly,
fly agaric mushroom, pyrite;
bottom row: Iris bud, detail of
a pink dianthus, red onion.

24

Nature is an infinite
sphere of which the
center is everywhere
and the circumference
nowhere.

Blaise Pascal

We all—as strange as it might sound—have "no-thing" in common. Humans, along with all things that make up our world, are made of particles at the center of which there is no-thing. That no-thing is symbolized by a point, a representation of both physical and nonphysical concepts, and that symbolic point is at the center of a mandala.

Points can transcend time and space, and, in this book, it is the point that sends us on a journey to explore how all things appear to spring from an origin to which we cannot point. That is why the first chapter is titled "Zero" and draws our attention to this very point. That said, our next step takes us to the circle—which is where the mandala comes in.

The center of the mandala, whether in its two- or three-dimensional representation or its conceptual expression (such as talking to make your point), is both its starting and ending point, yet *start* and *end* are locations that are theoretical and impossible to locate. That indefinable point is the place from which a mandala emerges.

There is also the matter of the center of time that is *now*, the moment from which all future moments unfold. Yet how can we point to now when, by the time we point to it, another now has already replaced it? While we cannot seem to find the absolute center points from which things spring, we do experience the things that appear to emanate from them. We cannot point to points, yet they appear to exist. It's enough to make your head spin.

Opposite: Abstract artwork.

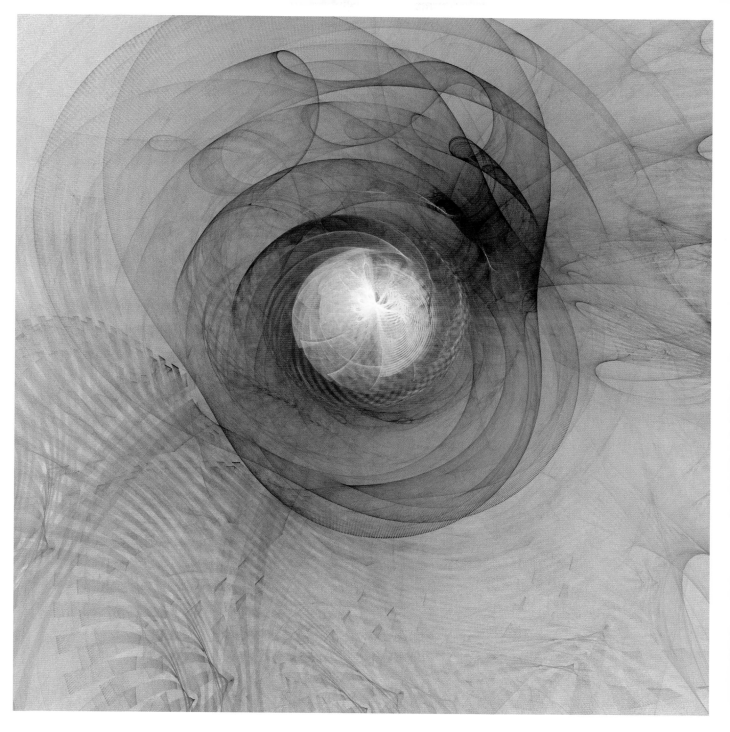

The most beautiful experience we can have is the mysterious. It is the fundamental emotion which stands at the cradle of true art and true science.

Albert Einstein

If books could be holograms, this book would be one. Each chapter contains parts of every other chapter. You can read about triangles in Chapter 3 and see a relation to fractals in Chapter 7. The book is literally a mandala—ideas and elements organized around the unifying core of the mandala. The point is to enjoy seeing connections between what you observe, both in this book and in your world—to see with new eyes.

Writing this book has been a journey in which each new fascination has led me to ask more questions. And I have found that the more questions I ask, the more amazing my journey becomes. I hope you'll have as much fun reading this as I had writing it! Bon voyage!

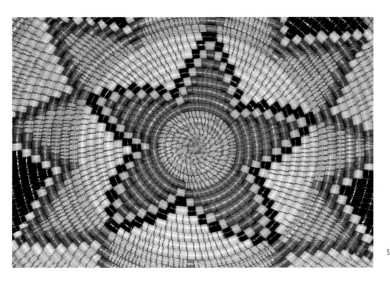

Left: Star pattern on a colorful hand-woven basket.

Opposite: Young gibbous starlet starfish, taken with a light micrograph.

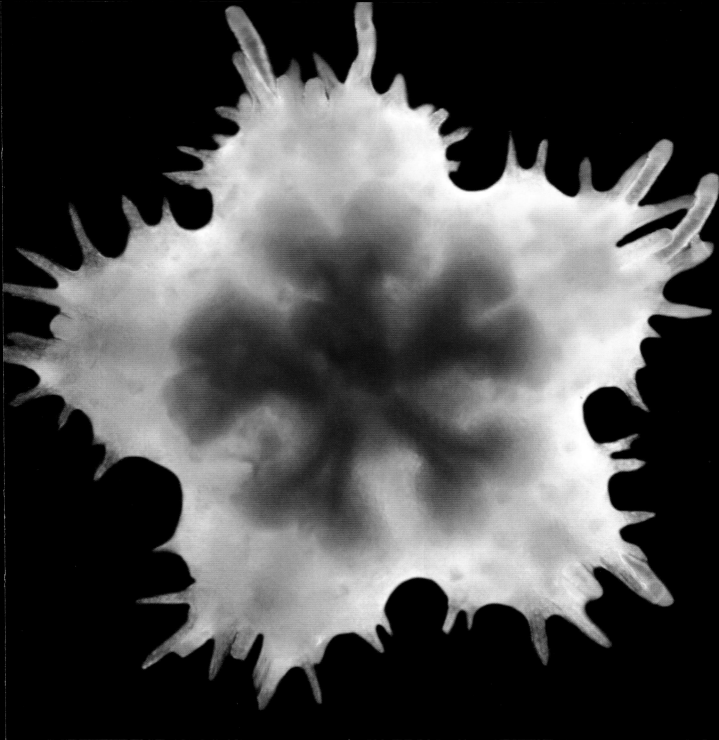

Nature itself rests on an internal foundation of archetypal principles symbolized by numbers, shapes, and their arithmetic and geometric relationships.

Michael Schneider

A CIRCLE FULL OF SHAPES

It is impossible to create perfect geometric forms with human tools; however, we *can* construct symbolic ideals of these shapes with a compass and straightedge. Two intersecting circles contain the proportions necessary to create simple, regular polygons such as those pictured here. Polygons (the name derived from the Greek *polygonon*, meaning "many angled") are two-dimensional shapes that can be seen in nature as well as in man-made objects. These diagrams illustrate the polygonal shapes we will examine in the following chapters.

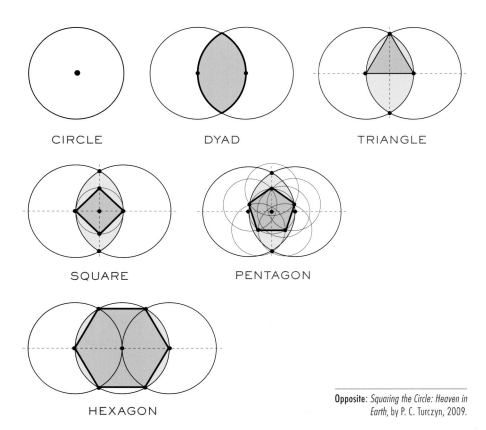

CIRCLE   DYAD   TRIANGLE

SQUARE   PENTAGON

HEXAGON

Opposite: *Squaring the Circle: Heaven in Earth*, by P. C. Turczyn, 2009.

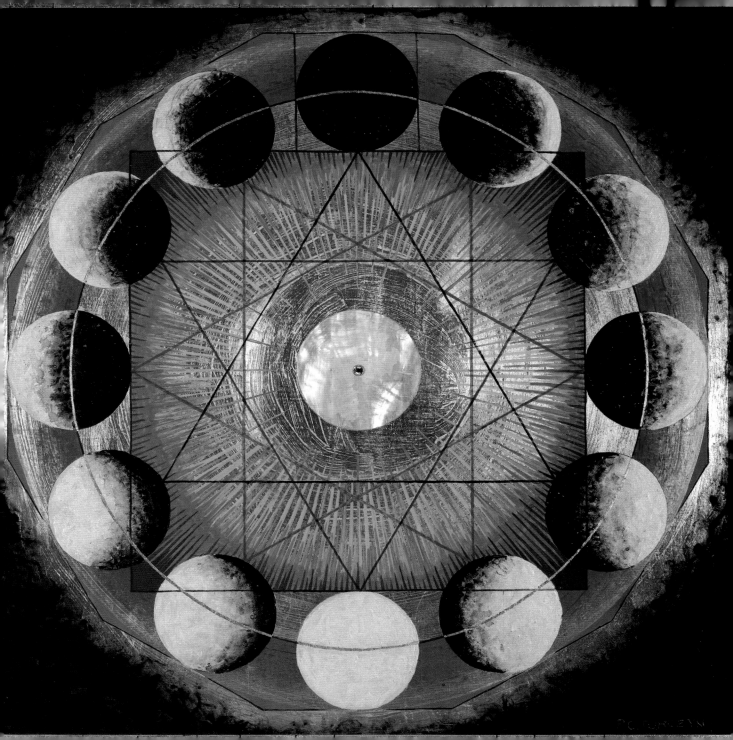

A Brief History of No-Thing

Our story does not have a beginning to which we can point, as it takes place in infinity. Further, it is a mystery that cannot be solved, a story in which we never find out who did it. But not to worry, there's plenty of drama to keep things interesting.

Even before we can entertain the concepts and actual things presented in this book, we need to start by talking about no-thing, that empty void we sometimes refer to as zero.

What we know as zero today has evolved through a long and controversial history. Following are just a few highlights from the fascinating story of zero.

Zero was not needed when life involved merely keeping track of numbered things such as time, flocks of animals, and possessions. If you didn't have something, you said it plainly and simply: "I don't have any." For the earliest of times, the lack of zero did not pose a problem.

By the second millennium BCE, however, zero had made its way into the sophisticated Babylonian numbering system and was represented by a space between "real" numbers as a placeholder. A tablet found in present-day Iraq, dated to 700 BCE, reveals a further evolution in the Babylonian system that used a symbol of three hooklike shapes to represent this no-thing placeholder.

Opposite: The high voltage emanating from the central electrode in a plasma lamp sends out plasma tendrils that seek the ground. The colors are a result of the relaxation of electrons in excited states to lower energy states after they have recombined with ions. These processes emit light in a spectrum characteristic of the gas being excited.

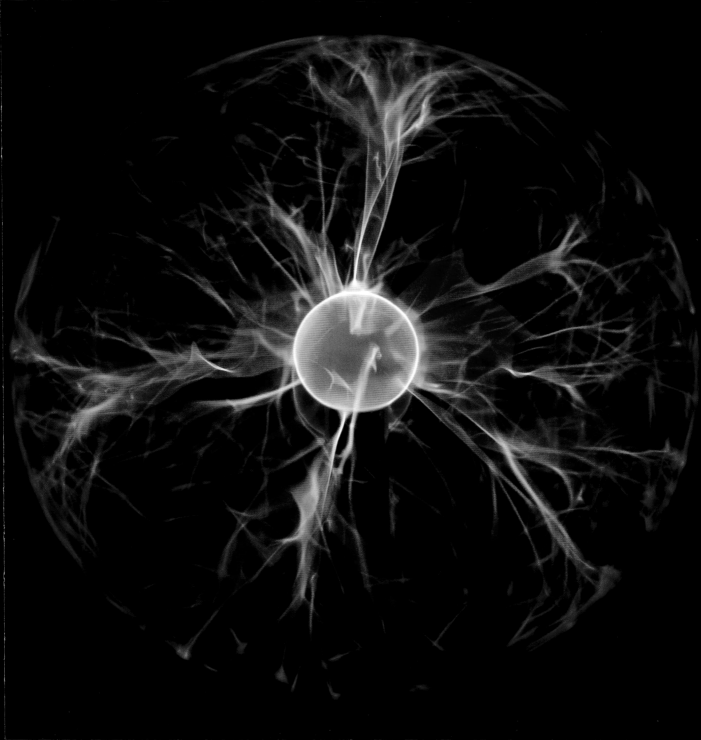

Nevertheless, the ancient Greeks were slow to embrace the concept of zero because, as they philosophically argued, "How can nothing be something?" The idea was actually considered dangerous. They believed that before the world had been created, there was a void from which chaos arose. The concept of no-thing was therefore associated with this void and chaos, and was to be avoided.

Zero does have some strange properties. Unlike other numbers, which when added to themselves result in a larger number, zero, when added to any number, does not change the number. It also refuses to play nicely with other numbers, insisting on "eating up" all other numbers by which it is multiplied, swallowing them up into its nothingness: $1 \times 0 = 0$, $2 \times 0 = 0$, $3 \times 0 = 0$, and so on. And division by zero is so problematic that it isn't even allowed! A variety of other troubling results revolve around mathematical equations involving zero, making it too scary to have been welcomed to the arithmetic party.

By around 300 BCE, the fearless Babylonians had taken zero a step further, now representing the no-thing placeholder with a symbol consisting of two slanted dashes, or wedges. Though it was not actually used as a number, it was the beginning.

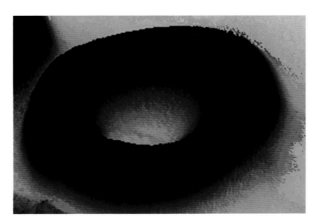

Left: 3-D atomic force micrograph of a red blood cell.

Opposite: Fried egg. The yolk appears as a singular point amid the egg white, yet in reality the yolk is composed of many particles whose structures consist primarily of empty space.

At the beginning of the beginning, even nothing did not exist.

Zhuangzi

While the origin of zero's use as an actual number is awash with controversy, some historians contend that it first took hold in India sometime before the eighth century CE. Buddhist and Hindu beliefs include a doctrine of emptiness called *nyat,* from which the Sanskrit word for "empty," *sunya*, is derived. Perhaps this belief paved the way to open minds about the idea of an infinite void.

In the late eighth century, a Persian mathematician, Muhammad ibn Mūsā-Khwārizmī, introduced the value of zero to the Islamic world. When zero arrived on the scene, the universe of mathematics and science blossomed in the Persian world. Centuries later, translations of his work made their way to the Western world.

Still, long after the collapse of the Greek civilization, the inability to accept zero as a number was retained by the West, delaying its incorporation into our numbering system. Further, in the Middle Ages, some Christians believed that since zero was not represented in the Christian Bible (or so it was thought), it ought not be used.

Above left to right: Point Zero in Paris marks the spot from which all road distances are measured in France; In Hinduism, marks on the forehead of both women and men can take the form of a dot (called a *bindi* when worn by a woman and a *tilak* when worn by a man). In Sanskrit, the word for "dot" or "point" is *bindu* and is used to symbolize the unmanifest form of the universe—the point from which form may emerge.

Opposite: The sun's corona is visible during a full solar eclipse in 2006, as seen in this photograph taken from Mt. Elbrus in the western Caucasus mountain range in Russia.

Zero, along with algebra and Arabic numerals in general, were decried by William of Malmesbury, a twelfth-century monk and English historian, as "dangerous Saracen magic." Unfortunately, the lack of zero prevented the growth of mathematics and science in the West. Without zero, numbers were held back from reaching their full potential.

In spite of religious and philosophical battles surrounding the use and acknowledgment of zero, progress and truth prevailed. As Charles Seife, author of *Zero: The Biography of a Dangerous Idea* (2000), put it, "Humanity could never force zero to fit its philosophies. Instead, zero shaped humanity's view of the universe—and of God."

What is the point?

"A cosmic paradox is at the beginning of all things," states Sri Aurobindo in his book *The Life Divine* (1949).

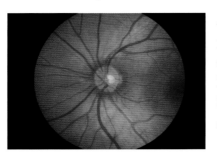

As if by magic, from the void comes the point, an object with zero dimensions, consisting of no length, volume, or area. It is essentially a primal shape that cannot be reduced into another shape and makes an all-around perfect symbol for zero.

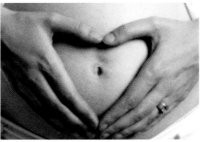

If you look at zero you see nothing; but look through it and you will see the world.

Robert Kaplan

Top left: Ophthalmic image detailing the retina and optic nerve inside a healthy human eye.

Left: The navel represents the connection between the child and its source of creation.

Opposite: Computer-generated image of sperms and egg.

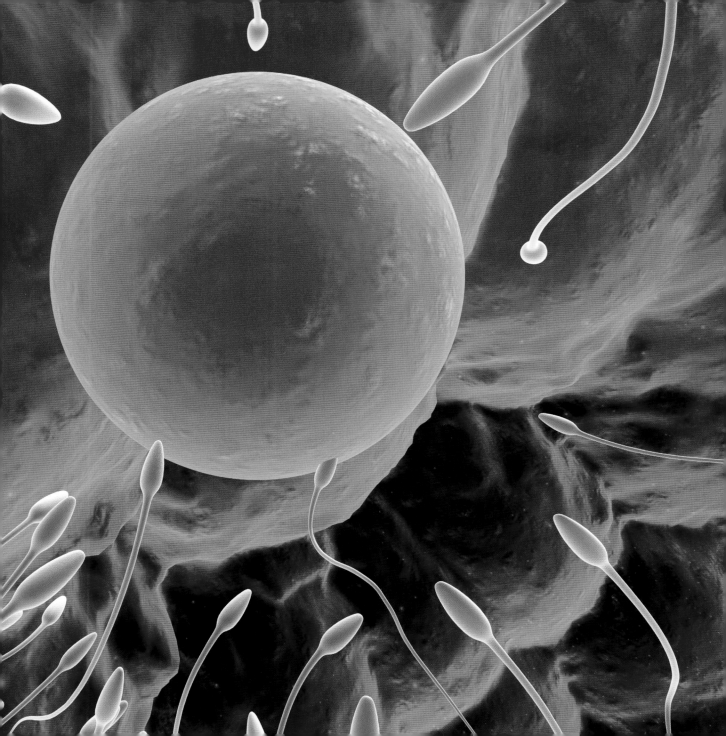

Upon zero we build
our systems of
reference, which is
merely a way of saying
that with nothing as
a center we have the
fulcrum for control of all
elaborations in form.

Franklin Merrell-Wolff

How does something come from nothing? That is the mystery in our "whodunit" story, but it doesn't stop us from trying to grapple with its understanding.

Imagine a blank blackboard symbolizing infinite emptiness. For the sake of this illustration, let's say the blackboard has no dimension or boundary—a concept that is, well . . . unimaginable. But bear with me—we are using finite devices to talk about infinity, and so our imaginations need to stretch a bit.

Our blackboard has nothing drawn upon it and has the potential of displaying infinite marks and shapes. On the board we draw an object—a point. By drawing a point, there is suddenly a distinction. There is a point and all that is not a point. However, while the point may appear to be separate from the blackboard, they are actually one and the same. The illusion that there is separation between the two is simply a distinction that we imagine between them. To understand this illusion of separation, consider two waves in the ocean. We might view them as individual, or even connected, but it is more accurate to see them as one ocean.

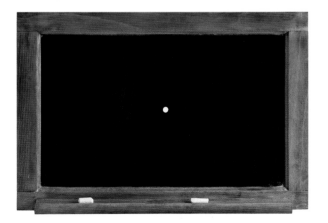

Left: Example of a point drawn on a blackboard, creating distinction.

Opposite: A drop of water cannot be separated from a lake, nor a wave from the ocean.

From this analogy we could say that from the infinite springs the finite, and both are unified in their apparent duality.

Why did the point first appear on the infinite blackboard? Well, you could say it was a thought that came out of nowhere, like the urge to eat a chocolate bar that suddenly pops into your head. Who knows where thoughts come from? It would seem that the answer to the question would also be the source of the question, which leads us in a circle—which rather appears like the infinite zero, doesn't it? That's something to think about.

ECUADOR
LATITUD: 0°- 0'- 0"
LONG. OCC. 78° 27'-8"

Left: The latitude of the equator is zero degrees and spans the land and/or territorial waters of fourteen countries, including Ecuador.

Opposite: In his book *Zero: The Biography of a Dangerous Idea* (2000), Charles Seife notes that "just as multiplying by zero causes the number line to collapse into a point, the vanishing point has caused most of the universe to sit in a tiny dot."

Circle

CIRCLING A ROUND

"Any way he looked at her she was perfect" is how the line described his love for the dot in Norton Juster's book, *The Dot and the Line* (2000). That's a dot for you—the point, the origin of all shapes, and perfect from all angles.

Just how did the circle get to be so perfect? Perhaps it's good breeding. To make a circle, you begin with a point—which, as we saw in Chapter 0, is actually a representation of the infinite.

While there may be a philosophic difference of opinion on whether numbering starts with one or zero, there is a general consensus that a circle, the first shape to emerge from a point, represents the concept of one. Just as the number one resides in all numbers, the circle contains the ability to create all shapes.

STARTING WITH ONE

To start our journey from one, we must come to terms with the fact that we are unable to know or point to what came before one. Like our inability to know what, if anything, existed just before the universe came into being, the origin of one cannot be determined, yet we can talk about what happened after we agree that one exists.

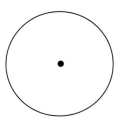

Opposite: Computer-enhanced linden tree stem cross section. Echoing the plant's initial growth—extending outward from a single seed—the plant stem reflects a structure based on growth expanding from a central core.

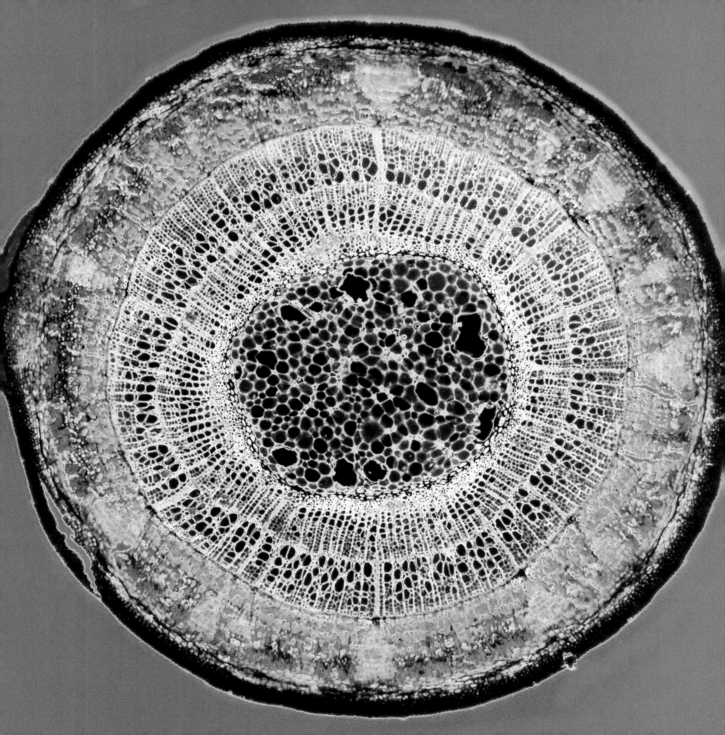

One has some interesting characteristics. Adding one to any number will change it from odd to even or vice versa (1 + 2 = 3, 1 + 3 = 4). Multiplied by itself, it always amounts to one (1 x 1 = 1). Multiplying any number by one does not change the number being multiplied (1 x 2 = 2). We can observe that one appears to have the ability to reflect both itself and other numbers, a trait that comes in handy when it begins the process of creating its offspring—shapes.

The circle is one of the first shapes we want to draw as children. We experience a certain delight in connecting a line to itself—one simple gesture that creates a whole thing, a shape that can represent any number of things from the sun to the wheels on a car to a lollipop. And then there's spinning in circles. Remember twirling yourself around until you were so dizzy all you could do was collapse on the ground and watch with wonder as the world whirled around you? Yes, circles affect us in many ways.

From all things one and from one all things.

Heraclitus

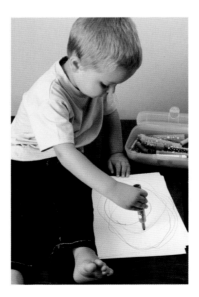

Left: Child drawing circles.

Opposite: Detail of *Resonance*, by P. C. Turczyn, 2008.

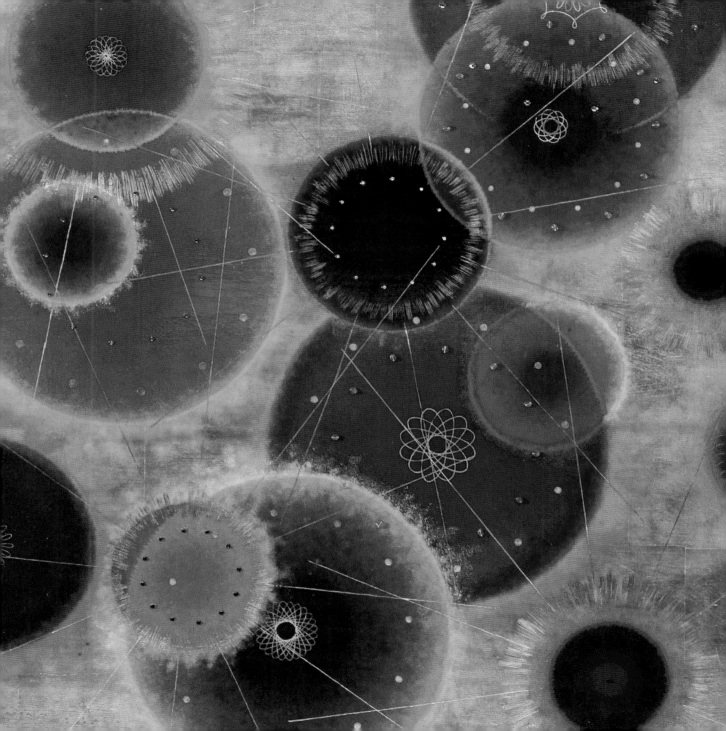

From ancient times, mankind has been aware of and attracted to circles, both as objects and as concepts associated with cycles of seasons and circles of friends. Ancient peoples used the symbol of the circle in rock carvings and often placed objects in a circular pattern. It is believed that the carvings may have symbolized the celestial bodies they observed in the sky, and stones arranged in circles, such as those found at Stonehenge, were perhaps used as aids in viewing them.

As we observe our world, starting from our own center, we see that we are surrounded by the primal pattern of the circle. Looking up to the heavens with a telescope, we see spherical objects moving in their circlelike orbits. Looking down, we see our feet planted on terra firma and experience the power of the earth's gravitational pull, drawing us toward its center. As we look around us, we see myriad things all made of atoms. Atoms themselves are mandalas composed of negatively charged electrons surrounding a central nucleus that contains a combination of electrically neutral neutrons and positively charged protons. And, of course, we are at the hub of all that we see—we, too, are at the center of our own mandala.

> The world is single and it came into being from the center outwards.
>
> Joannes Stobaeus

Left: Located in England, Stonehenge is perhaps the world's most famous prehistoric structure. Built by Neolithic and Bronze Age peoples from ca. 3000–1600 BCE, the stones—some of which weigh up to fifty tons—are arranged in a circular pattern. Stonehenge, scholars have recently theorized, likely functioned as a familial burial ground; others believe it was an astronomical observatory.

Opposite: Horseshoe Bend near Page, Arizona. The bend of the Colorado River around the central rocky hub gives this natural feature a circular quality.

To observe and contemplate the many examples of the circles in our lives offers us the opportunity to consider our place in the universe as well. We come to know the world by first experiencing ourselves as separate from others. While we may ultimately strive to see the world as a unified entity, it seems that the recognition of ourselves as seemingly independent is a necessary step to achieving a broader perspective. But all that musing and investigating comes only when we are ready to see our way back to where things began—the primal one.

THERE'S A HOLE IN THE WHOLE

At the center of a circle lies a secret: it's empty! To create a circle, we pivot a compass around a point, and—voila!—a circle appears. But then it gets interesting. If we examine the point, defined by *Merriam-Webster* as "a geometric element that has zero dimensions and a location determinable by an ordered set of coordinates," we find nothing. To illustrate this anomaly, we can make a dot with a pencil and subject it to magnification. First we'll find carbon molecules. Further investigation leads to the discovery of invisible atoms, followed by quarks, which are moving points of energy that cannot even be illustrated in diagrams. At every stage in our examination, we find the boundaries defining each object continually dissolve, leaving us with a "something" that has no boundaries. What does this mean? Where does it end? Are we looking into infinity?

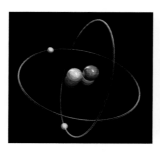

Left to right: Computer-generated image of a helium atom. Helium is composed of two electrons orbiting a nucleus, which contains two protons and two neutrons; Carbon atoms. Although this image is an artistic rendering, it uses original 3-D topographic data taken with an atomic force microscope.

Opposite: This circular stone archway is a natural feature in Monument Valley, Utah.

There is no actual point to which we can point. It appears that the yellow brick road of exploration takes us to an ineffable place, leading us to conjecture that all things finite are made up of the infinite. Extrapolate that and you have a heady realization: our finite bodies infused with and connected by points of infinity.

While these points of infinity cannot be found, they are a part of all things, appearing everywhere in every moment. They are the pivotal center upon which all things are made and provide visual doorways into the unknown, appearing as trees, rocks, and even in the faces of our loved ones. At any moment we can look right in front of ourselves and consider the implications: We are, in fact, looking at representations of the infinite through the display of oneness.

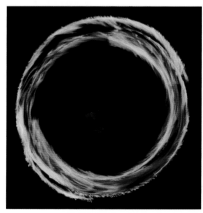

Top left: Cultures of *Phomopsis*, a destructive plant fungus.

Left: A sparkler spinning in a circle around an imaginary center illustrates how activity can create appearance of some-thing—a circle that revolves around, or evolves from, no-thing, the infinite point. But note that there really is no circle, only the appearance of one.

Opposite: Yellow lichen growing in a ring on a stone.

The soul is a circle.

Plato

We cannot find anything at the center of a point, yet we know that it takes a point to make something. Without the atom that springs from the infinite point, there would be no things. The same is true in the world of geometry. All shapes spring from an original point. They may become other shapes such as triangles or squares, but their beginnings always point to an original source and center. As Lao Tzu puts it in the *Tao Te Ching*, "Thirty spokes join at one hub, yet it is the emptiness inside the hub that makes the vehicle useful."

The pattern of a mandala or circle is implied in the nature of all things, whether or not the boundary perfectly describes a circle. Electrons, one of the most fundamental parts of matter, surround a nucleus. From the point there is the ability to expand, and expansion, at least initially, is in the shape of a circle. In his book *Inventing the Circle: The Geometry of Nature* (2003), Johan Gielis puts forth a mathematical formula that shows how symmetrical shapes can be generated from the circle. His Superformula "provides a way to define a unique geometry for each Supershape, from which all other shapes can be defined."

Left: Dharma Wheel on Jokhang Temple in Lhasa, Tibet.

Opposite: Gills on the underside of a mushroom.

From the one came the two, came the three, came the 10,000 myriad of things.

Tao Te Ching

When the pattern of the circle becomes mobile, things get even more interesting. As atoms come together to form molecules, they arrange themselves into visible substances that can become physical objects. Residing within every object is the circle parent, as seen in the structure of the atom, passing on its pattern to its heirs, a pattern that is a reflection of—you guessed it—the infinite.

Though the substance of things is created around no-thing, we do have a some-thing. And this some-thing is the mandala, the pattern that informs the creation of all the stuff of the universe. Circles, spheres, cylinders—all represent patterns that emanate from the infinite point. All things in the universe dance around a common theme: the circle, first ambassador of the infinite.

THE HERITAGE OF THE CIRCLE

In nature, we see that certain characteristics can be passed on to later generations. So it is with the circle and the point from which it springs. The point represents duality since it signals the illusion of the first step away from the infinite, though as we saw in Chapter 0, the point *is* the infinite. As an extension of the point, the circle reflects the illusion of the point's dual nature while simultaneously embodying the singular nature of oneness and unity. The attribute of unity is reflected in the circle's perfect rotational symmetry—the ability to rotate around the central point while remaining the same. The quality of duality can be seen when the circle expands or contracts in size radially—changing sizes negates its perfect symmetry. Nonetheless, despite its dual nature, it is the agreed-upon symbol of oneness and unity.

Opposite: Architectural mandala. Concentric circles combine with equilateral triangles to create a lacy structure.

Number proceeds
from unity.

Aristotle

Why and how the circle duplicates itself is a mystery, but when it does, it infuses its property of symmetry, along with the magical spark of the infinite point, into the shapes that follow. From atomic structure to objects we can actually see, all phases point to the inherent symmetry of the original source of the perfect circle. Therefore, in observing any object, we can imagine its links with the past, present, and future—the quality of symmetry inherent in all things, regardless of their outward appearance. The recognition of this continuum can augment our ability to experience our true nature, our integral connection with wholeness.

The circle is a blueprint representing how the universe works: All things revolve around a center; all things have a point or they do not exist. All things are made up of mandalas.

Clockwise from top left: Orange sulphur shelf mushroom growing in forest; Artichoke coral; Apricot.

Opposite: Detail of a gazania flower.

There is in reality neither truth nor error, neither yes nor no, nor any distinction whatsoever, since all—including contraries—is one.

Zhuangzi

Above: Ponte de São Gonçalo Bridge in Amarante, Portugal.

Opposite: Morning Glory Pool, a hot spring in the Upper Geyser Basin of Yellowstone National Park, in Wyoming.

My life is an indivisible
whole, and all my
attitudes run into
one another; and
they all have their rise
in my insatiable love
for mankind.

Gandhi

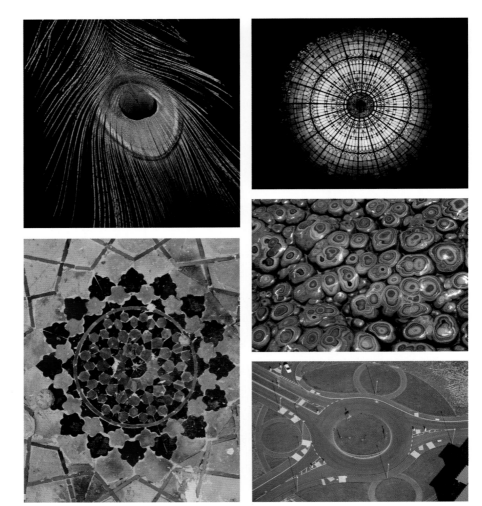

Clockwise from top left: Detail of a peacock feather;
Stained-glass dome in unknown location; Detail of
green malachite; Aerial view of a traffic roundabout;
Mosque dome in Bukhara, Uzbekistan.

Opposite: Crystallized vitamin C, taken with a light micrograph.

Whence shall he have grief, how shall he be deluded who sees everywhere the Oneness?

Isha Upanishad

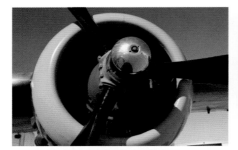

Clockwise from top left: Aircraft piston engine; Detail of grape hyacinths; Pipes of a community heating system under construction—cylinders are a basic shape that can be visualized as dragging a circle in a straight line; The London Eye (the largest Ferris wheel in Europe, built in 1999 to celebrate the new millennium).

Opposite: Detail of tunicate, or sea squirt, sacs. The tunicate is a simple marine animal. These were found in the seas near Indonesia.

CONCENTRIC CIRCLES

OVER AND OVER AGAIN

Can the flap of butterfly wings in Brazil set off a tornado in Texas? We can't be sure, but the theory well illustrates cause and effect, as do the ever-expanding concentric circles caused by a stone tossed into a pond.

The term "butterfly effect" was first used in 1969 by meteorologist Edward Lorenz to describe the idea that small acts can create large results. Just as a tossed pebble sends ripples through the surrounding water, we too create similar effects when we engage in the act of smiling or saying a kind word. Concentric circles spread our essence out into the world, overlapping and rippling with the rest of humanity—all of us experiencing the effects of each other in our lives.

José and Miriam Argüelles describe a mandala in terms of the pattern of concentric circles: "A mandala consists of a series of concentric forms, suggestive of a passage between different dimensions. In its essence, it pertains not only to the earth, but to the macrocosm and microcosm, the largest structural processes as well as the smallest. It is the gatepost between the two."

Opposite: *The Monad: Oneness*, by P. C. Turczyn, 2008. Expanding equally in all directions from a central point, all circles are identical in shape, representing the undivided universe and wholeness. The artist used proportions of the golden mean (see Chapter 5) to plot the sizes of the circles, giving them a sense of growth and endless expansion.

Remember there's no such thing as a small act of kindness. Every act creates a ripple with no logical end.

Scott Adams

Concentric circles share a common center or axis. In three-dimensional form, concentric patterns can be seen in the shapes of spheres, tubes, and cylinders. Imagine those nested cups kids play with—they create a cylinder with concentric circles when put together. Patterns of concentricity are also seen in nature as rings radiating outward in a cross section of tree trunks, marking the trees' growth in the same way as the antlers of some animals do. Even in the bones of dinosaurs, rings indicate growth rate.

The pattern of concentric circles is played out on a grand scale in the multiple orbits of planets around the sun, as well as in the orbits of stars around a central mass in a galaxy. The rings that circle around Saturn are composed of ice and rocks that form circular gaps within the rings. Jupiter, Uranus, and Neptune also have rings, though not as pronounced. On a personal level, we have our own orbits in which our lives revolve around a person, family, group, or even a cause. And there are those that orbit us as well—friends and loved ones who see into our centers and appreciate who we are at our core.

Left: Computer-generated image of Saturn. Among Saturn's most remarkable features are its concentric rings, located in the plane of its equator and comprised of ice particles, rocky debris, and dust.

Opposite: Geode stone sliced to reveal rings of color.

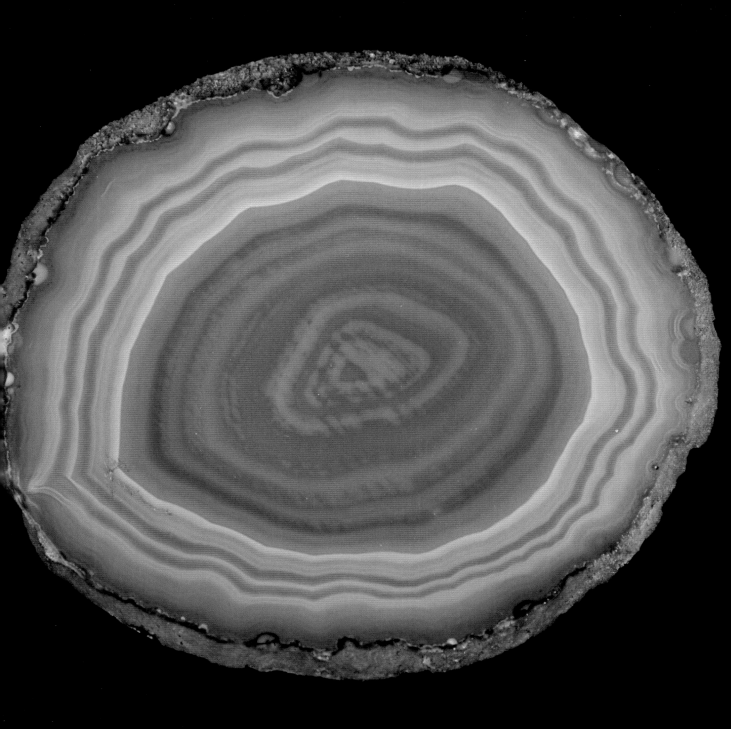

Like ripples in a pond, each awareness-moment expands out from its own center, containing in its form-pattern the configuration of all phenomena in the universe, material and immaterial. And so the process of centering—the gathering of oneself as if by an inward throw of a stone into the pool of one's own consciousness—is also a Mandala.

José and Miriam Argüelles

Clockwise from top left: Multicolored arcs of a double rainbow hint at a concentric circular pattern; Peleides blue morpho butterfly; Sliced leeks; Green bracket fungi, also known as shelf fungi; Lens from a lighthouse—the Fresnel lens was invented for lighthouses and requires less material than a conventional lens due to its concentric angled rings.

Opposite: Concentric circles expand outward from the impact of a water droplet on the surface of a pond.

In helping others, we shall help ourselves, for whatever good we give out completes the circle and comes back to us.

Flora Edwards

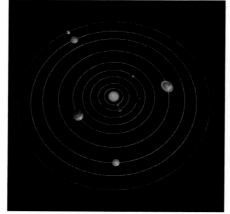

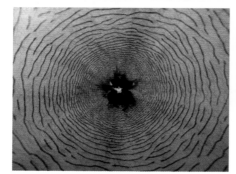

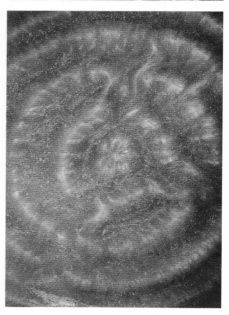

Clockwise from top left: Detail of a sliced red onion; Old brick roof forming concentric circles; Detail of freshly-cut beet; Macro shot of a carrion plant; 3-D computer rendering of the solar system—our solar system is comprised of planets and moons that travel in orbits around a central sun, creating paths very similar to concentric circles.

Opposite: The rings of a pine tree track its yearly growth.

Whatever affects one directly, affects all indirectly. . . . I can never be what I ought to be until you are what you ought to be. You can never be what you ought to be until I am what I ought to be. This is the way the world is made. . . . This is the interrelated structure of reality.

Martin Luther King Jr.

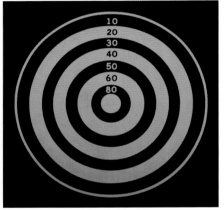

Clockwise from top left: Detail of 3,000-year-old Native American petroglyph carved in red sandstone in the American Southwest; Circular terraces found in the Inca ruins of Moray, Peru, were possibly used to observe how climatic conditions affected crops; The rings of a dartboard zero in on the prized center; Dome of the Mughni Church in Ashtarak, Armenia — the presence of three concentric circles is believed to represent the Holy Trinity.

Opposite: Concentric patterns on a tortoise shell.

Spheres

IN A PERFECT SPHERE

Humans are attracted to spheres. After all, spheres have surrounded us for as long as we can remember. Ancient peoples etched circles into rocks to represent the celestial spheres they observed in the sky, and today we chart the ones they were not even able to see. A lunar eclipse can lure even the most dedicated couch potato outside to witness the event. And we still make wishes when we are moved by the sparkling presence of the North Star.

Spheres symbolize and actualize unity with dimension. Expanding in all directions from its center, the sphere represents mandalic wholeness in three-dimensional fashion. As with the circle, a sphere requires that every point on its surface area be equidistant from its center.

The cosmic world offers a variety of examples of circular and spherical traits. Celestial bodies form themselves with the gravitational pull toward their center while rotating in spherical symmetry. Some have rings or attract moons to circle them while orbiting the sun. The development of spherical geometry enabled ships to better navigate around the planet. It is even conjectured that the universe itself might be circular in nature.

Opposite: The familiar sphere we call our moon.

First of all, we must note that the universe is spherical.

Nicolaus Copernicus

On our own planet we are witness to smaller, but no less grand, examples of the sphere. We begin our lives in tiny eggs, growing outward in a symmetrical fashion. The openings on our bodies are circular in nature, and we come equipped with spherical eyeballs through which we visually absorb the multifaceted visuals of life—images that are, as we'll recall from earlier in this chapter, all related to the circle.

A SPHERE OF POSSIBILITIES

Spheres are comfortable and safe. Many animals take advantage of the sphere's ability to offer the least surface area for the most interior space by curling into themselves to stay warm or to defend themselves from predators. The sea anemone reaches out from its center to collect food, then recoils into the smallest ball-like form possible when it senses danger. We humans enjoy rolling ourselves up into a fetal position for a nap as we once did in our mother's womb.

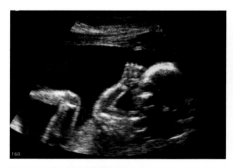

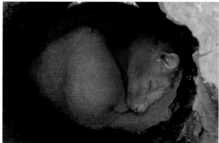

Clockwise from top left: Sonogram of a human fetus; Pearl in an oyster; Ringtailed possum curled up for a nap in a log.

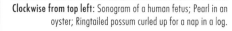

Opposite: Clown fish and withdrawn sea anemone.

The pursuit of truth and beauty is a sphere of activity in which we are permitted to remain children all our lives.

Albert Einstein

Spheres are fun. They bounce; they roll and bowl. Spheres make good all-around toys for young and old. Because of its symmetry, with every surface point being equidistant from the center, a sphere is good at rolling in any direction—balls have been used in games by humans since ancient times. Soapy bubbles delight children when blown through wire frames, and raindrops can mesmerize us as they cling to a leaf. Each is formed when surface tension struggles to reduce the surface area, creating a spherical shape.

Spheres are likable. Tom Hanks's character in the movie *Cast Away* created his own relationship with a sphere—perhaps the rounded nature of the volleyball that became his surrogate buddy, Wilson, was the quality that made it especially endearing.

Spheres are indispensable. One sphere we all have in common is the one on which we stand. It provides a place to eat, sleep, live, and love—it's home.

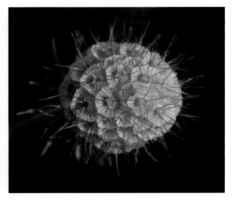

Clockwise from top left: Soccer ball; White drumstick primula; Young girl blowing bubbles—a spherical shape is formed when surface tension struggles to reduce the surface area of a bubble.

Opposite: Dew droplets on a leaf.

We sail within a vast sphere, ever drifting in uncertainty, driven from end to end.

Blaise Pascal

Clockwise from top left: Cluster of green grapes; Onion flowers; Marbles; Barrel cactus; Detail of the Atomium in Brussels, Belgium—built for the 1958 Brussels World's Fair as a symbol of atomic structure.

Opposite: Growing cabbage.

An attempt at visualizing the Fourth Dimension: Take a point, stretch it into a line, curl it into a circle, twist it into a sphere, and punch through the sphere.

Albert Einstein

Top: Balls of blue azurite and green malachite.

Center from left: Vancouver's TELUS World of Science geodesic dome; Astronomical observatories on a mountain at night, unknown location.

Bottom from left: Sea urchin; Robin's eggs in a nest.

Opposite: Unopened blue globe thistle.

There is no change,
and no anarchy, in the
universe. All is system
and gradation. Every
god is there sitting in
his sphere.

Ralph Waldo Emerson

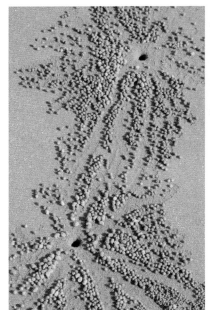

Clockwise from top: Silhouette of a dandelion; Orb-weaver spider and
its web, pictured on the Uluguru mountains in Tanzania; Sand "bubbles"
outside the burrow of a sand bubbler crab. After sifting through sand it
has collected in search of microscopic food, the crab forms the unused
grains into spheres that it tosses behind its legs.

Opposite: Moeraki Boulders on the Otago coast of New Zealand. The
spherical boulders are a type of concretion that have been exposed by
the erosion of the mudstone that envelops them.

Eyes

LOVE AT FIRST SIGHT

Looking into the eyes of our beloved, we are drawn into circles of love. Our eyelids form a rounded embrace for a sphere that, in turn, holds on its surface the circular iris surrounding a circular pupil. With such intricate design, no wonder we enjoy looking deeply into the eyes of another person.

With eye contact comes the possibility of seeing into the heart of another as well as seeing eye to eye. When our eyes meet another's gaze, a connection is made, enabling us to see more than what's visible, to perhaps see into each other's soul. Such depth of feeling has inspired poets and songwriters to pen sonnets and lyrics of love.

Eyes serve us in many ways. In the preverbal courtship rituals of Western cultures, an intense gaze into the eyes of an attractive potential mate can last two or three seconds. Depending on what the viewer beholds, the pupil dilates, indicating interest, while the lenses become thicker or thinner to accommodate focus. If attention is returned, the heart beats faster, and it's off to the races!

Eye contact can give other signals that demand various responses, whether positive or negative. We say "Look me in the eyes" when we want someone's full attention, and we warn misbehaving children, "I'm keeping my eye on you!" A confrontation between two animals can involve a stare-down, while one animal avoiding eye contact can signal submission or anger.

Opposite: Tokay gecko eye.

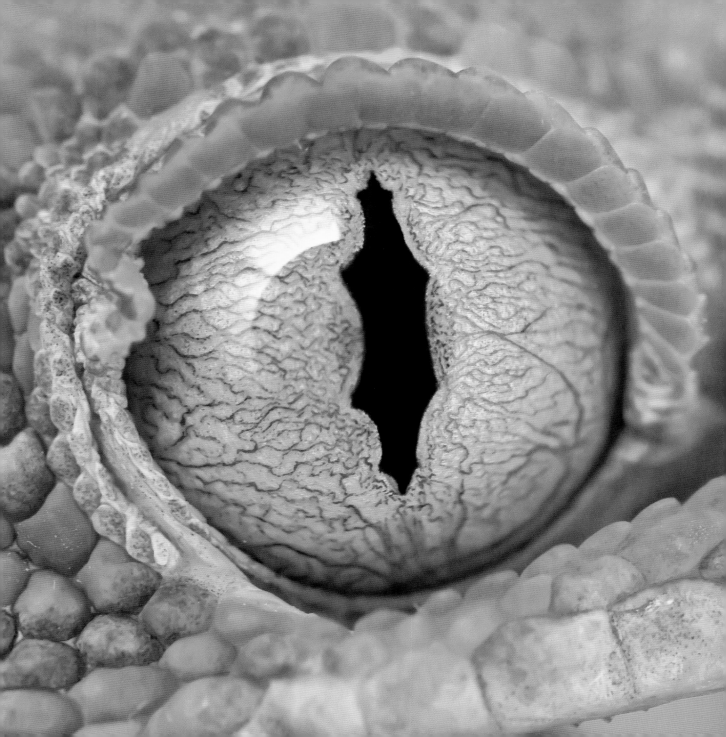

The eye is the first circle; the horizon which it forms is the second; and throughout nature this primary figure is repeated without end. It is the highest emblem in the cipher of the world.

Ralph Waldo Emerson

AN EYE FOR EVERY NEED

Eyes come in a variety of shapes, from simple to complex. Single eye structure, like that of humans, is found in vertebrate animals and employs just one lens to fine-focus images onto the retina. Binocular vision (when visual fields overlap, as with human eyes) offers depth perception and generally occurs in animals that need to see what they are pursuing, whether a tasty meal or a comely mate.

Nocturnal vertebrates, such as cats, have eyes composed primarily of rod cells, making them more sensitive to light than those of humans. Reptiles require eyes placed on the sides of their heads, since they need to have a broader visual range for ambushing their prey.

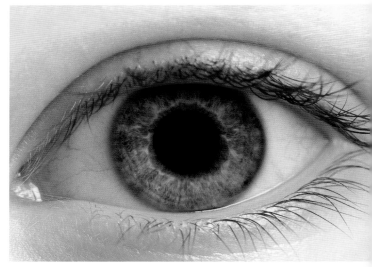

Above: Human eye.

Opposite—top row: Tarsier, starry puffer fish, crested crane; **center row:** Zebra, reef fish, Chinese water dragon; **bottom row:** Red-eyed tree frog, giant moray eel.

I shut my eyes in order to see.

Paul Gaugin

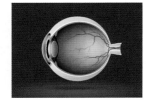

Most crustaceans and insects have compound eyes, which have multiple lenses and sometimes consist of thousands of individual photoreceptor units that provide a wide-angle view to detect quick movements. Many winged insects require three-dimensional vision to enable them to fly at high speeds, and scientists believe some are able to see up to three hundred frames per second, compared to humans, who can see approximately sixty frames per second.

SEEING WITH CIRCLES

The very organ with which we perceive our visual world, a composite of infinite circular particles, is itself a spherical shape.

"We do not know why eyes are round," says professor Larry S. Liebovitch, PhD, but "we know *how* they are round." In his article "The Shape of the Eye: Why the Eye Is Round," published in *Advances in Organ Biology: The Biology of the Eye* (2006), he examines various possibilities that might explain the circular nature of eyes.

Far left: The very organ with which we perceive our visual world is itself a spherical shape.

Above: Great grey owl.

Opposite—top row: Western green mamba, peacock, beagle; **center row:** Veiled chameleon, emerald tree monitor, light refraction on a camera lens; **bottom row:** Red-and-green macaw, emerald damselfly.

The eyes, those silent
tongues of love.

Miguel de Cervantes

The basic structure of the eye involves opposing forces that create roundness. The outward force exerted by the pressure of the liquid *aqueous humor* inside the eye is balanced by the inward tension of the eye's surface layer, similar to the air within bubbles that seeks release but is contained by its stretchy film exterior.

The seemingly obvious reason that eyes are round is to facilitate rapid eye movement. But this reason does not hold completely true since, depending on the needs of the creature, eyes operate in many different ways, with only mammals having the rapid and accurate movement facilitated by a spherical mechanism. While there appear to be a variety of possible reasons for eye roundness, none provide complete satisfaction.

Above: Parrotfish.

Opposite—clockwise from top left:
Siberian cat; Young white-headed marmoset; Rainbow lorikeet; Turtle; Tropical butterfly; Iguana.

The eyes have one
language everywhere.

George Herbert

Dr. Liebovitch concludes that, "Neither optical, nor movement, nor structural, nor evolutionary, nor developmental reasons seem to be the primary reason why the eye is round." He says, "The evolutionary record is whispering to us that eyes were round before they moved rapidly or accurately."

There is something about the primal shape of a circle that enables animals to see a world that is itself a reflection of the circle. Could there be some connection between the shape of our eyes and the circular nature of life itself? We don't really know, but it's interesting to consider.

Far left: Buddha eyes painted on a stupa on the Swayambhunath Temple in the Kathmandu Valley, Nepal. The "Eyes of the Buddha" symbolize the omniscience or all-seeing nature of the Buddha.

Above: Toucan.

Opposite—top row: Eagle owl, soldier fly, octopus; **center row:** Discus fish, Asian elephant, grasshopper; **bottom row:** Sandhill crane, crocodile.

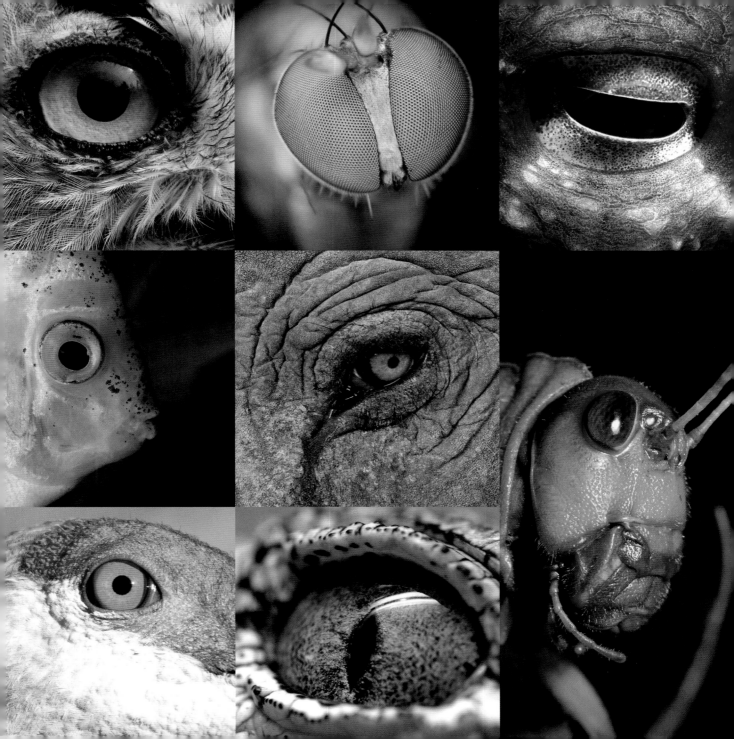

Radials

EXPLODING FROM THE CENTER

Radial explosions grab our attention. When elements expand and radiate outward from a central point in a symmetrical pattern, such as the pyrotechnics in fireworks displays, involuntary *oohs* and *ahs* erupt, while images of atomic bomb blasts illicit horrifying yet equally captivating reactions. A kaleidoscope fascinates us while simultaneously pulling us in and spinning us out with expanding patterns of symmetry emanating from a central point. Starburst shapes surrounding words such as "New!" and "Improved" on consumer product labels are designed to catch our eye. Images of energy bursting from a central point surround us and often astound us.

Why do we find ourselves so captivated by the pattern of a starburst? Could it be that it speaks to some deeper part of our nature, an aspect of ourselves that intuits a connection to inward and outward expansion? Perhaps it is a primal connection to some aspect of creation, or even a spark of the infinite.

A BURST OF NATURE

The outreach of a flower's petals might catch the eye of a passing bee. The spines of a porcupine form a sphere of weapons, ready to unleash a spray of barbs at a moment's notice. Even our eyes radiate intricate patterns in our irises, expanding from the pupil, drawing in the gazes of others.

Opposite: Macro shot of a dandelion, tinted blue.

The quietest poetry can
be an explosion of joy.

James Broughton

In the underwater world, starfish reach out their "arms" to express the starburst pattern of a radial explosion, while sea urchins with spines attached to their sticky tube feet remind us of porcupines. The dried shell of the urchin reveals a fivefold radial symmetry called *pentamerism*.

The undulating tentacles of the sea anemone collect and deposit food collections into its centrally located mouth. Aptly named for the multipetaled flower, anemones are actually corals and are from the phylum *Cnidaria*, which stems from the Greek word for "nettle." With its tube-shaped body firmly anchored by its sticky foot, it captures its prey and defends itself with an army of tentacles surrounding its mouth.

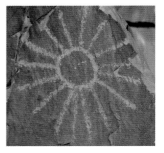

Right top to bottom: Close-up of a sea urchin skeleton; Petroglyph sun on a red rock in Saguaro National Park, Tucson, Arizona; Beams from the Umpqua River Lighthouse, on the Oregon coast; Carved stone Dharma Wheel on the Sun Temple at Konark, Orissa, India, built in the thirteenth century.

Opposite: Sea anemone.

Laws are essential
emanations from the
self-poised character of
God; they radiate from
the sun to the circling
edge of creation.

Theodore Roosevelt

These images illustrate the sunburst quality of
the radial pattern.

Top: Dome of the Hungarian Parliament Building
in Budapest—one of Europe's oldest legislative
buildings and the largest building in Hungary;
center row: Bromeliad, eleven-armed sea star;
left: Fourteenth-century sundial in Bouzov
Castle, Czech Republic.

Opposite: Shining sun.

Just as a flower gives
out its fragrance
to whomsoever
approaches or
uses it, so love from
within us radiates
towards everybody
and manifests as
spontaneous service.

Swami Ramdas

Top: Fireworks over Prague Castle in the Czech Republic during New Year's celebration.

Above left to right: Horsetails, ornamental kale, cactus.

Opposite—top row: Green and pink plant, variety unknown, purple sea cucumber with orange tentacles, green spider chrysanthemum; **center row:** Orange and white gazania flower, whale's tongue agave plant, white and pink water lily; **bottom row:** Yellow sea anemone, green and red succulent, purple pennywort.

As in an explosion,
I would erupt with all
the wonderful things
I saw and understood
in this world.

Boris Pasternak

Clockwise from top left: Rotunda of the Michigan State Capitol
building; Dome of the Cathedral of Brasília, in Brazil; Detail of
main dome of Selimiye Mosque in Edirne, Turkey; Interior of a hot
air balloon; Columns and skylight of an arch in Moscow.

Opposite: Human iris.

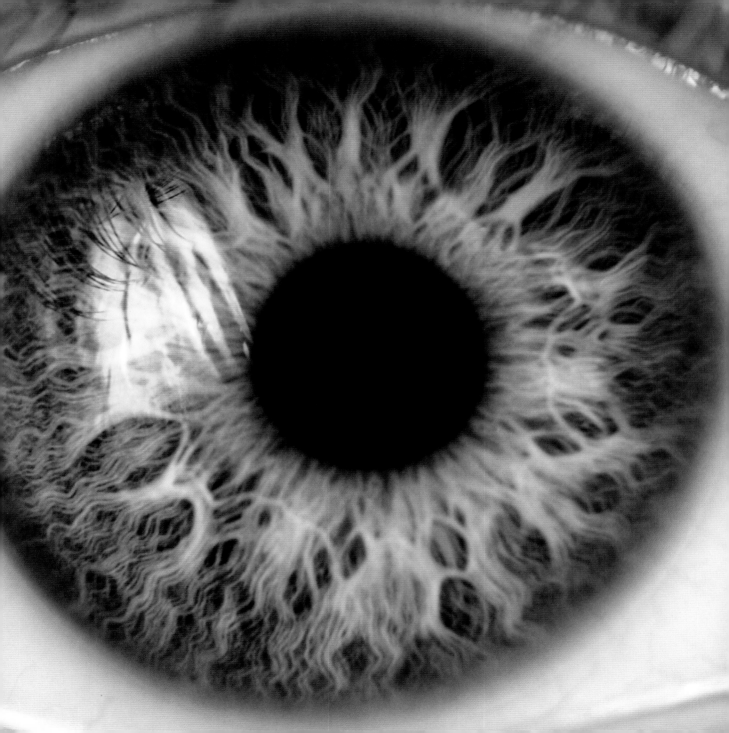

The wise man looks into space and does not regard the small as too little nor the great as too big; for he knows that there is no limit to dimensions.

Lao Tzu

Clockwise from top: Two pinchusion protea flowers; Sea urchin; Tree porcupine sleeping on a branch in Trinidad; West Indian lantana.

Opposite: Colony of zoanthids.

Dyad

DUALITY TAKES SHAPE

The circle is a symbol of "one-ness." It contains no differences within itself, for in every direction leading outward from its center it is the same. While generally recognized as a symbol for unity and wholeness, the circle's emergence from the infinite indicates time, distance, and therefore separation (what is within the circle as opposed to what is not). Perhaps it is this quality of duality—the ability to convey both wholeness and separation—that contributes to its mysterious ability to self-reflect, to make two.

All shapes spring from the womb of the circle, beginning with the *dyad*, an almond shape that represents the duality of two. Through the geometric process of creating a dyad—also known as a *mandorla* or *vesica piscis* (a Latin term meaning "fish bladder")—we witness the transformation from one to two and from two to many. The creation of distinctive things begins in the dyad.

With the dyad comes our ability to know one thing from another. Light is not known as such without darkness. We can only discern that something is cold when we are able to discern that another thing is hot. Duality allows us to identify separate things, to distinguish *this* from *that*, subject from object. Objects that appear in consciousness can only be understood or contemplated when there is a relational opposite to which they can be compared. When One

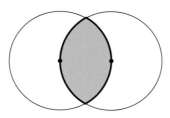

Opposite: A ripening almond is the shape of the *vesica piscis*, also known as a *mandorla*, which is Italian for "almond."

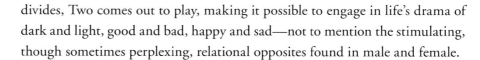

divides, Two comes out to play, making it possible to engage in life's drama of dark and light, good and bad, happy and sad—not to mention the stimulating, though sometimes perplexing, relational opposites found in male and female.

The paradox of Two is that it springs from the ineffable, singular One. As we explore the shapes and numbers to follow, we must remember that they all derive from the point to which we cannot point, the infinite place wherein all things reside and from which all things spring. The array of phenomena we see—a face, a car, a cloud—are not separate from the infinite whole, just as waves are not separate from the ocean.

MAKING TWO

The dyad comes into being when two identical circles overlap. To create a dyad, the circle must first divide itself through the process of reflection. Just as we see ourselves in a mirror yet know that the two-dimensional reflection is not real, the reflected circle is but an illusory replica of the first. The mirror image that is created, though appearing identical to the original circle, is, in fact, an illusion—just as the point from which the circle sprang is also an illusion. It may have all the characteristics of its source, but it is not the source. And, as we remember from Chapter 1, the circle itself is a reflection of the infinite point that cannot be found, the no-thing. As Parmenides, an ancient Greek philosopher, said, "Everything is of the nature of no thing."

Left: Colored transmission electron micrograph of methicillin-resistant *Staphylococcus aureus* (MRSA) bacteria.

Opposite: Immunofluorescence light micrograph of skin cells that have resulted from one cell dividing into two, a process known as mitosis.

"In the beginning God created heaven and earth," that is, the first fall of all is from the One into Two, from unity into number, from what is perfect, undivided and indistinct into imperfection, division and distinction, and from the whole into parts.

Meister Eckhart

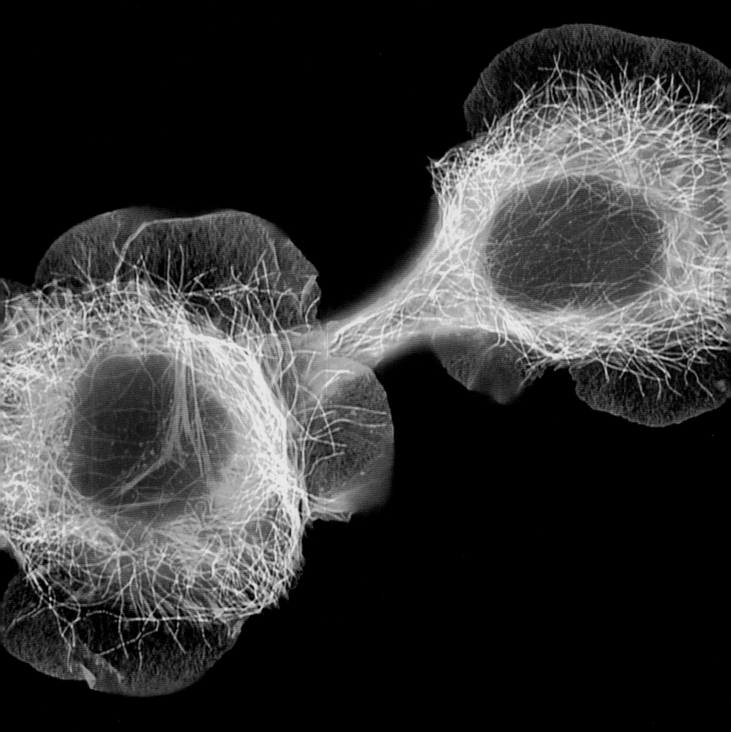

If there be light, then
there is darkness; if
cold, heat; if height,
depth; if solid, fluid;
if hard, soft; if rough,
smooth; if calm,
tempest; if prosperity,
adversity; if life, death.

Pythagoras

The dyad does not inherit perfect rotational symmetry from the circle, as only 180-degree and 360-degree rotations can create reflections of themselves (figure 2-1). However, within the dyad there exists the potential to dissect a line (figure 2-2). This is accomplished by drawing lines between the central points of each parent circle, followed by drawing a line between the two points created where the circles intersect. The ability to divide is yet another trait that reflects the illusion of duality or separation. The lines serve to distinguish *this* from *that* and represent polarity—good/bad, harmony/discord, unity/diversity.

Two-ness brings to mind examples of coming together—as in pairs, duets, or twins. It also speaks of coming apart—as in divisions, divorce, and disagreements. There often appear to be two sides to an argument, and relationships certainly have ups and downs. It is not unlike a marriage between two people that can be blissful and/or miserable. With two comes the possibility of relationship: it takes two to tango as well as tangle.

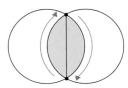
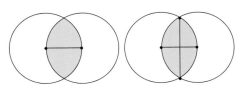

FIGURE 2-1   FIGURE 2-2

Above left to right: The dyad can be rotated at 180 and 360 degrees to create a reflection of itself; Within the dyad is the potential to dissect a line.

Left: The *vesica piscis* shape, or dyad, can be seen throughout the Chalice Well Gardens in Glastonbury, England. Pictured here is the Chalice Well cover that, according to Christian myth, marks the site where the chalice containing drops of Christ's blood from the Crucifixion was placed. Some believe that the almond shape symbolizes an aspect of the Divine Feminine.

Opposite: Light microscopy of alga showing binary fission (asexual reproduction via cell division).

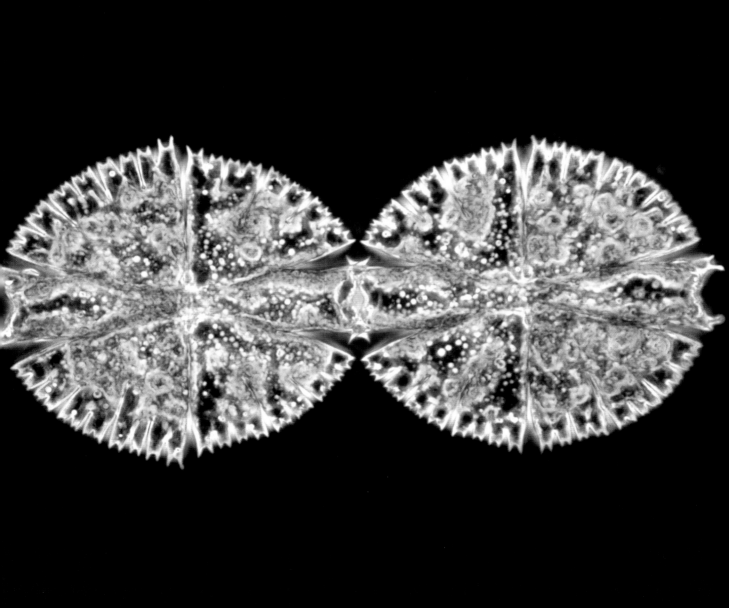

POLARITIES UNITE

Polarity is an essential ingredient for creation and growth. As with a magnet, the pull between the dyad's positive and negative poles represents the urge to bring opposites together to regain the state of unity found in the parental circle. The dyad seeks balance and yearns for the center, for the middle ground. On a universal scale, we might even see our longing to find or remember unity as a tension between the parts and the whole.

In his book *Dictionary of Symbols* (1998), Carl Liungman states, "The world's most basic relationships are perceived as a balancing act between two opposing life forces, yin (the white) and yang (the black)." The dyad is a symbol that clearly illustrates the play of opposites. The qualities of male and female, known as *anima* and *animus* to Jungian psychologists, contribute to the development of relationships between women and men and the potential of their coming together to create a child. The combination of water and light causes a seed to sprout, whereas the contrast of light and dark creates visible images.

Our true self is a mirror which contains all things.

Arthur Edward Waite

Above left to right: Stone ornament with dolphins in Sodwana Bay, KwaZulu-Natal, South Africa; Two goldfish swimming in circles. *Vesica piscis*, a fishlike shape, literally means "bladder of a fish."

Opposite: While the yin yang symbol, featuring the two opposing elements of dark and light, is generally thought to illustrate the dual nature of reality, harmony, and balance, it also represents wholeness, since the elements are contained within a circle. We live in a world composed of opposites that can only exist in the context of the finite world in which they appear. As a drop of water is not separate from the ocean, duality is not separate from the infinite.

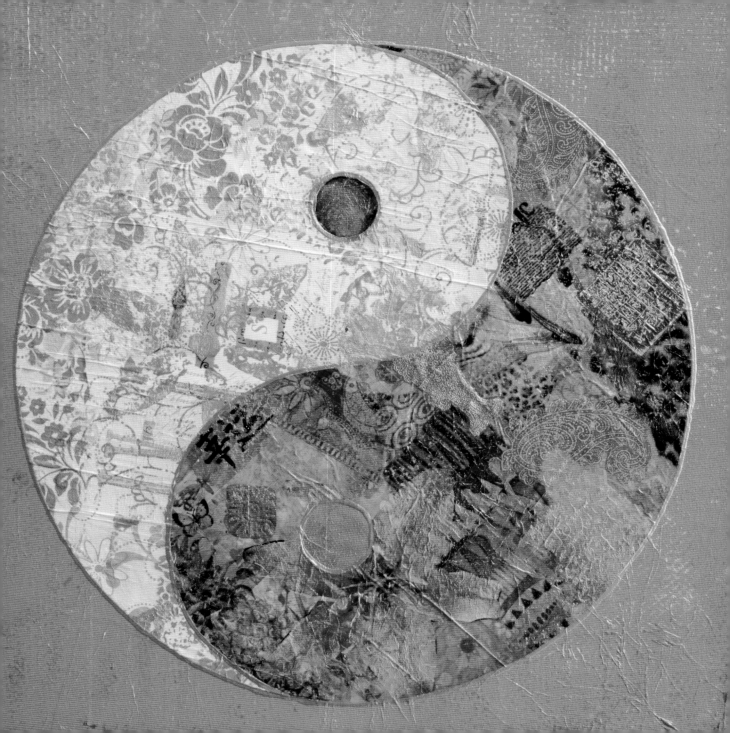

Atomic structure offers yet another classic example of united polarities: the composition of the hydrogen atom. One proton with a positive electrical charge combined with one negatively charged electron make an elemental building block of our material world. Together they create the only atom having two components, and—as with the dyad—their partnership is just the beginning of more things to come.

GROWING WITH TWO

Duality offers entertainment and the opportunity to distinguish good from bad, real from unreal. Movies would not hold our attention if the drama of dark and light did not exist in some way. If Dorothy only picked flowers along the Yellow Brick Road without battling the Wicked Witch of the West, we would snore our way through *The Wizard of Oz*. So it is with our lives. Without the challenges offered by duality, life would be quite dull. Living would seem pointless, and—as we know from observing the message of the mandala—without a point, nothing exists.

Engaging the tension held between opposites enables us to grow. Finding our center entails a process of inquiry that discerns what is from what is not. If we take time to consider the effects of two-ness in our own lives, we observe that belief in duality apart from wholeness is a cause of our suffering. When we see ourselves as totally unique and separate from our primal source of unity (or whatever we choose to call it), we feel terribly alone. But, just as the dyad is not separate from but a part of the circle, we too are connected to the whole universe. To be un-holy (not whole) is to be living under the illusion that we are separate from the whole.

Symmetry is the archetypal key that unlocks the true nature of the world.

Thomas McFarlane

Opposite: Mushrooms grow in the cavity of a tree trunk.

Really, the fundamental, ultimate mystery—the only thing you need to know to understand the deepest metaphysical secrets—is this: that for every outside there is an inside and for every inside there is an outside, and although they are different, they go together.

Alan Watts

We begin the journey of individuation as infants, coming to terms with our apparent separation from the "other." Later, in coming to terms with the illusion of separation, we may finally arrive at the beginning point and realize that we are in fact not separate from One, but *are* One. In a sense, we are shapes that have emerged from the dyad yet are also reflections of the infinite point, endowed with the urge to find balance, to return to unity and oneness. It is a sense of completeness as represented by the mandala that we seek in life.

The world offers infinite possibilities to explore what is real and what is not. For centuries, mystics of all religious traditions have employed a practice of inquiry to explore the duality of our experience. It is through that process of questioning that we begin to find answers, which in turn lead to more questions, which can then ultimately point to the fundamental truth that there is only one primal source of everything.

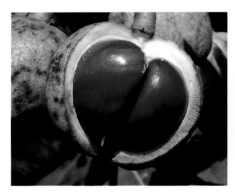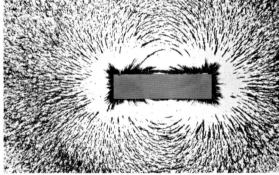

Above left to right: Twin chestnuts; Bar magnet with iron filings, showing magnetic field pattern.

Opposite: Sliced fresh tamarillo, or Dutch eggplant.

TWO AND MORE

Within the dyad lies the possibility of more. If we have two, what happens if we add them together? The dyad gives the first indication that there is more than one and there may be more to follow.

The *vesica piscis* can be seen as a "form generator" from which "all the regular polygons can be said to arise," states Robert Lawlor in his book, *Sacred Geometry: Philosophy and Practice* (1989). The dyad has been used to symbolize the feminine principle of reproduction and is associated with divine or virginal births. The almond-shaped doorway through which babies are born is the portal through which we pass to embark on life's journey.

The infinite point that is both everywhere and nowhere finds new expression in the shapes that spring from the dyad. Regardless of how complicated or multifaceted the following shapes appear, each one possesses the ability to reflect its parent, the circle.

The root of all things is difference.

Ibn al-'Arabī

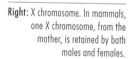

Right: X chromosome. In mammals, one X chromosome, from the mother, is retained by both males and females.

Opposite: Colored scanning electron micrograph of a freshwater diatom showing the exterior of a cell wall shaped like a dyad. Diatoms are unicellular, photosynthetic algae, of which there are about 100,000 species.

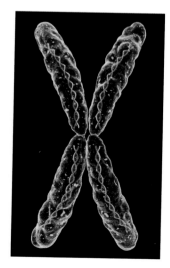

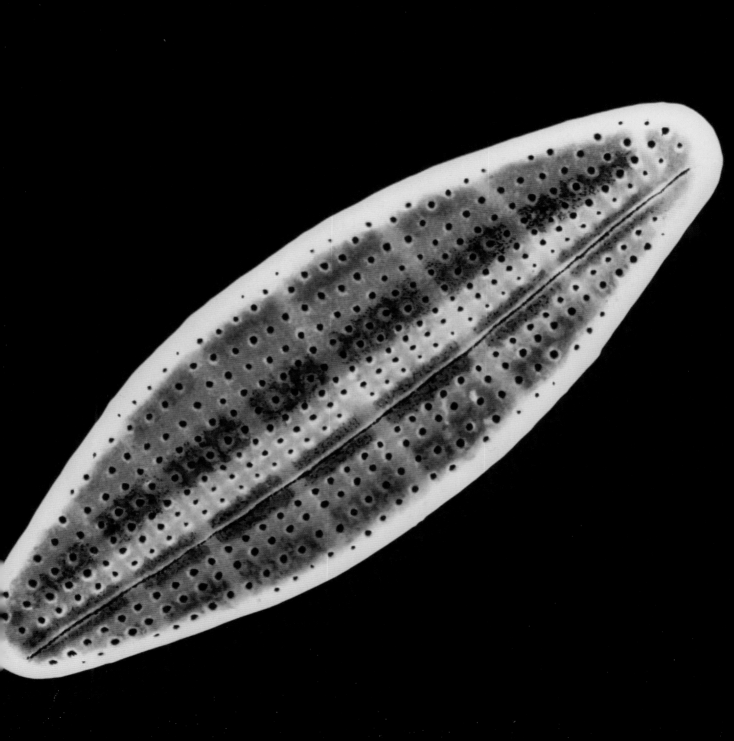

Words create
distinctions,
and distinctions
create dualities.

Joel Morwood

Clockwise from top left: An American football is egg-shaped for aerodynamics, making passing between players easier; Stained glass window in a church, featuring a nativity scene. The shape of the dyad, or *vesica piscis*, is used in Christian art to symbolize Jesus Christ; Lithops, or "living stone" plants, are succulents that grow pairs of thick leaves resembling stones; Burj Al Arab, a luxury hotel in Dubai, United Arab Emirates.

Opposite: Purple and green orchid.

BILATERAL SYMMETRY

Geometrically speaking, bilateral symmetry can be defined as symmetry in which similar parts are arranged on opposite sides of a median axis so that only one plane can divide the individual into essentially identical halves. Symmetry brings to mind the beauty and harmony of balance seen in nature. It is a pattern with which we, as humans, are very familiar. When we come face to face with a friend, we are looking at an example of bilateral symmetry—the left and right sides of the friend's face are mirrorlike images, or reflections, of each other. Humans and most animals are bilaterally symmetric, as are some flowers and most leaves of plants.

While drawing a line down the middle of something appears to create two separate entities, it is important to note that these are imaginary distinctions that are in fact parts of a whole. As the fifth-century Greek Neoplatonist philosopher Proclus stated, "The cosmos is not a unity here and a plurality there, but a unity and a plurality at the same time throughout its whole being . . . and there is nothing you can take within it that is not both one and many." As with waves in the ocean, the universe and everything in it are parts of an indivisible whole.

Right from top: Crown-of-thorns or Christ plant; Ladybug.

Opposite—clockwise from top left: Close-up of a plains zebra in South Africa; Peacock butterfly; Bee's head; Barn owl taking flight; Raindrops on a leaf; Fruit from a coco de mer palm tree, native to the Seychelles archipelago (the fruit is known as the sea coconut).

TRIANGLE

READY, SET, GO

By breaking through the polarizing boundaries of two, we arrive at three. By engaging the tension held between two entities (as represented by the dyad), there results a third that reunifies its makers, as in the joining of male and female to create a child who unites the threesome as a family. No longer my way or your way, this way or that way, a third way is introduced: *our* way. With three comes a sense of completion that signals resolution; one and two are united in three.

The potential to create more is inherent in both one and two, but it is not until a third element is added that the world begins to unfold in a continuing pattern. Carl Jung describes three as "an unfolding of the One to a condition where it can be known—unity becomes recognizable." The triad is the first shape to emerge from the dyad; it is composed of three lines and contains three angles.

Three, when seen as a trinity, has an important place in a variety of religious doctrines. In Christianity, it is the unity of the Father, Son, and Holy Spirit and is considered the expression of three persons in one Godhead. For Hindus, the trinity concept is revealed in the displays of creation, maintenance, and destruction, personified in the forms of Brahma the creator, Vishnu the preserver, and Shiva the transformer. All three are considered to be manifestations of one reality. One of several Buddhist representations of a trinity is the threefold embodiment of reality: the *dharmakaya*, body of ultimate truth; the *sambhogakaya*, body of light and joy; and the *nirmanakaya*, the conditioned human body. As with the Christian and Hindu traditions, these three aspects of being are considered indivisible.

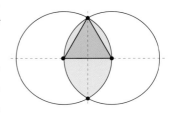

Opposite: The three seed pods of a pansy flower.

128

The Triad has a special
beauty and fairness
beyond all numbers,
primarily because it is
the very first to make the
actual potentialities of
the Monad.

Iamblichus

SYMMETRY IN MOTION

As we recall, the perfect and whole circle duplicated itself through the process of reflection to create the duality necessary for reproduction. Those two circles combined to create the dyad: one whole and one reflected, illusory whole. The process of duplication results in the creation of the dyad, a distinct object that inherits three traits: wholeness and symmetry from the original circle, and a quality of illusion from the second, reflected circle. These three traits are passed on to the third shape, the triad. The ongoing productions of shapes are continued reflections of the original union: all are whole, yet simultaneously illusory. The symmetry of the dyad, triangle, and shapes that follow, though limited in comparison with the circle, point to the ever-present spark of perfection that is inherited from the parent circle.

As an equilateral shape, the triangle is composed of three equal sides. It does offer variations on a theme in the form of its cousins, the isosceles triangle (two sides of equal length) and the scalene triangle (no sides of equal length). Each variation contains the three points and three sides that make them knowable as representations of the triad.

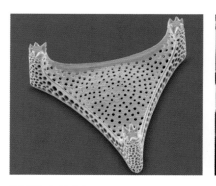 

Above left to right: Colored scanning electron micrograph of a diatom; Daylilies in a garden. The triangular, three-part nature of the lily ovary is reflected in the flower's six petals, which form two interlocking triangles.

Opposite: Microscopic cross section of a lily ovary.

130

A cord of three strands is not easily broken.

Ecclesiastes 4:12

STABLE AND ABLE

Unlike its circular parent, the triangle does not enclose the largest space within the smallest perimeter; among all convex polygons, it encloses the smallest amount of space within the largest perimeter. The triangle shape that results from three parts leaning on each other is structurally strong and stable. By unifying its three sides, the triangle relieves the tension of opposing forces to create a solid structure that requires no external support. This attribute is the reason why an equilateral triangle cannot be easily deformed and can add stability to other shapes. For instance, a brace placed diagonally across the middle of a parallelogram will create two triangles, resulting in a more stable structure and preventing an overweighted square from collapsing. Triangles are used to brace structures by adding more support, just as our triangular pelvis supports our body, and the A-frame truss is used in architectural structures.

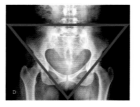

Clockwise from above: The structural stability of the triangle makes it a perfect shape for a truss. The shape of the triangle will not change when all the lengths and sides are fixed, unlike a square, which requires the additional fixing of its angles; The Louvre Pyramid in Paris, France (1988), designed by I. M. Pei, contains seventy triangular glass segments; The shape of the human pelvic bone is triangular.

Left: Reverse side of the Great Seal of the United States. The seal appears on one-dollar bills. In 1782, Secretary of Congress Charles Thompson is believed to have said that the pyramid represents "Strength and Duration."

Opposite: The Great Pyramids at Giza, Egypt, are each composed of four triangles with a square base.

Every rectilinear surface
is composed
of triangles.

Plato

The strength of the triad can also be seen in human social structures. In tribal communities the chief, shaman, and tribal members comprise a tripartite group that has provided a successful and stable cultural structure for many centuries. The American government has been designed with three branches of power to ensure that checks and balances maintain the triadic system. Within most religious organizations, the triad structure comprises the doctrine, the spiritual figurehead, and the congregation. Body, mind, and spirit describe our personal, unified expression of One.

Our continuing exploration and research into the development of shapes might be seen as following the smaller and smaller rivulets that branch out from the source of the flow—the center of the circle. While the ongoing appearance of shapes and patterns emanating from the circle add interest to what we see in the form of things, we should remember that what we are viewing is a reflection of the infinite point. Yet, in true mandalic fashion, all things are ultimately organized around a unifying center.

Left to right: Pyrite. The octahedral structure displayed here is composed of eight triangular faces; Pink fringed tulip, also known as a crispa tulip.

Opposite: Tourmaline. Tourmalines often form elongated crystals with roughly triangular cross sections.

Learn from yesterday, live for today, hope for tomorrow. The important thing is not to stop questioning.

Albert Einstein

Top left to right: Geese migrating in their traditional V-formation; Triangles have been used as a symbol for fire, perhaps because triangles suggest volcanoes or the teepee-like shape of the hearth fire. They are also used to symbolize caution.

Left: A triquetra—a symbol composed of three interlocking *vesicae piscis*— on a ca. eleventh-century runestone located in the park of Uppsala University in Sweden. The triquetra can also be seen in Celtic art, as well as in rock art that predates Christianity.

Opposite: Volcanoes in Bromo National Park in Java, Indonesia.

But every tension of opposites culminates in a release, out of which comes the "third." In the third, the tension is resolved and the lost unity is restored.

Carl Jung

Top: Triangular piles of salt on the surface of the Salar de Uyani salt lake in Bolivia.

Center: Blue morpho butterfly.

Bottom, left to right: Arc of a modern suspension bridge in Toronto, Ontario, Canada; View from a window of the Chrysler Building in New York City; Exterior of the Chrysler Building, showing the triangular windows.

Opposite: Sailboat.

THREESOMES

Three-ness surrounds us, from the natural world we see, to sayings we hear and concepts we experience. Three breaks through and transcends the opposites contained in the dyad, joining all together in a relationship of wholeness. With three comes a sense of completion and even comfort—not too hot, not too cold, but just right. We learn the ABCs, not the ABs; we knock thrice, not twice; and a sports fan's cheer doesn't stop at "go" or "go, team," but exclaims, "go, team, go!" When it comes to expressing the quality of completeness, triads just feel right. Listed here are just a few examples of three-ness—surely you'll have some to add of your own.

Body, mind, spirit

Truth, beauty, goodness

Beginning, middle, end

Past, present, future

Birth, life, death

Ready, set, go!

Three basic planes: above, surface, below

Types of rocks: igneous, metamorphic, sedimentary

Hegel's thesis, antithesis, synthesis

Freud's id, ego, super-ego

Action, reaction, result

Three notes in a triad—the most basic form of any chord

A human ear's three semicircular canals

The middle ear's three ossicles—the three smallest bones in the human body

Three Fates and Three Graces

Three strikes and you're out

Faith, hope, charity

Of the people, by the people, for the people

Above, from top: Triad of a mother, father, and child; Three Wise Monkeys—Kikazaru hears no evil, Mizaru sees no evil, and Iwazaru speaks no evil.

Opposite—top row: Dragonfly on a blade of grass. Insects are comprised of three basic body parts—head, thorax, and abdomen; Three medals—gold, silver, and bronze—are awarded to the top three contestants in a competition; The *Three Legs of Mann* (1979) by Bryan Kneale is a bronze sculpture outside the Ronaldsway Airport on the Isle of Man. The national symbol of the Isle of Man is a triskelion of three bent human legs; **center row:** Red bell pepper composed of three inner chambers; Butterfly iris (which has three different sets of petals); The structure of most atoms consists of three particles: protons (yellow) and neutrons (blue) comprise the central nucleus, which is orbited by electrons (green); **bottom row:** Heartsease or Johnny-jump-up; The three primary colors—blue, yellow, and red—can be mixed in various combinations to compose all other colors; Computer-rendered cross section showing the three main components of the earth—crust (light orange), mantle (dark orange), and core (red).

Square

FOUR ON THE FLOOR

With four comes solidity and stability. While the perfectly symmetrical circle represents heaven, the stable square represents the solid nature of the earth. We tend to like this shape for making things we count on for nonchanging attributes. The world offers many examples of the square in action: Four-legged critters roam the earth, while four-legged chairs support our bodies. Our hearts have four chambers and the human body has four systems: nervous, respiratory, circulatory, and digestive. Cities often employ a square grid pattern for laying out streets, and baseball fans enjoy warm summer days watching people run around a square diamond. With feet squarely planted on the ground, we use the four cardinal directions as indicated on a compass—north, south, east, and west—to perceive and organize the space around us.

Four symbolizes a solid foundation and the desire for security and safety in the stability of nonchange. Buildings are squarely set on rectangular foundations. Who wants to rock and roll in an earthquake? Stable squares can be hard to move, but they do have their plusses and minuses. We have solid and substantial square meals and square deals. But people who exhibit behavior that is conventional, or slow to change, are labeled as square.

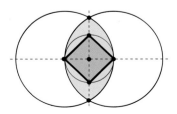

Opposite: A four-leaf clover, thought to bring good luck to the person who finds it. According to Irish legend, each leaf represents something beneficial: the first is for fame, the second is for wealth, the third is for love, and the fourth is for health.

The right thing is to
proceed from second
dimension to third,
which brings us,
I suppose, to cubes
and other three-
dimensional figures.

Plato

Another representation of four is carbon. Elemental for life forms on our planet, carbon is in the makeup of both the earth and our bodies. The number of chemical bonds formed by atoms in carbon is—you guessed it—four. The tetrahedral (four-sided) structure of carbon creates a diamond, the hardest material that occurs naturally. The same holds true for tetrahedral-shaped silicon, a compound that makes up the majority of the earth's crust.

SQUARES ILLUSTRATED

Residing in the square is a cross, made by either drawing lines from corner to corner or side to side. It symbolizes relationship and integration, as in the way that the warp and weft of cloth combines elements from two different directions to create an integrated whole, and has been used to represent the four cardinal points as well as the four elements. Vertical and horizontal lines have been used to show the relationship between the divine (vertical) and the earthly (horizontal). In mathematics, the cross represents addition, though turned at a 45-degree angle it represents multiplication. It also symbolizes division—the intersection of longitudinal and latitudinal lines divides the earth into four quadrants.

When used in gestures, the sign of the cross has cultural significance. Some sects of Christianity trace the symbol of a cross in front of their bodies in a ritual hand motion that symbolizes the trinity of the Father, Son, and Holy Spirit. Another sign of the cross is employed when one is promising to tell the truth, as in "cross my heart, and hope to die."

The humanitarian organization of the Red Cross employs the cross in their logo as a symbol of aid that is available to all, regardless of national or political borders. It is also used as a symbol of aid in the medical world, where it can be seen on first aid kits and the uniforms of caregivers.

Opposite: Blossom of a dogwood tree.

144

The human heart is like a ship on a stormy sea driven about by winds blowing from all four corners of heaven.

Martin Luther

Though frequently associated with Christianity, the cross has been in use as a symbol since ancient times and has figured in many religions and belief systems. It was used in ancient rock carvings as a symbol of the sun, and appears in the Egyptian Ankh and the Native American Medicine Wheel. The swastika, which contains a cross in its center, had been used by many cultures before the Nazis corrupted it during Hitler's regime.

In Tibetan Buddhist mandalas, the symbolism of four is rich in meaning. Such concepts as the four boundless thoughts of loving kindness, compassion, sympathetic joy, and equanimity are built into the image of a square "cosmic" palace. The mandala palace is a sacred image that may be represented two-dimensionally, in paintings and sand mandalas, or three-dimensionally, in sculpture and architecture.

Other religious traditions also incorporate the square in their sacred art. Southwest Native Americans such as the Navajo, whose sand paintings are remarkably similar to those of the Tibetan Buddhists, create healing mandalas for people who are ill. After a period of purification, a tribal medicine man creates a sand mandala in whose middle, after completion, the sick person sits. After a ceremony, the sand painting, considered toxic because it absorbed the illness, is swept away, similar to rituals practiced by Tibetan monks to symbolize impermanence (see Introduction, page 8).

Opposite—clockwise from top left: Celtic stone cross; Arabic tile in the Alhambra in Granada, Spain; The swastika (from the Sanskrit svastika) symbol is pictured here on an old Buddhist sanctuary wall in Japan. Before its association with the Nazis in the early twentieth century, the design was widely used by many cultures and religions around the world to represent positive qualities, often symbolizing universal harmony or four cardinal points. Today, the symbol continues to be used in various traditions; Square-shaped spiral petroglyph at the V-Bar-V Heritage Site in the Verde Valley, Arizona.

SQUARING OF THE CIRCLE

Circles were considered sacred shapes by ancient peoples and symbolized the infinite and divine, such as the circular orbits of heavenly bodies. Squares represented the "foursquare" solid nature of earth, material reality, or human-kind. A process known as "squaring the circle" metaphorically describes the paradox inherent in reconciling the infinite and the material world. Challenged to construct a square that is equal in area to that of a circle (using only a straightedge and compass), one finds this task is geometrically impossible. This is because the circle is incommensurable, impossible to mea-sure. (While mathematics does allow for close approximation by squaring the radius and multiplying the result by pi, pi represents an infinite rather than concrete number.) The impossibility of squaring the circle symbolizes the relationship between the infinite nature of the circle and the concrete nature of the square. Yet when an equal comparison is approximated, the infinite can be expressed through the finite, as can be seen in architecture and art.

Swiss psychoanalyst Carl Jung felt that a mandala illustrated the squaring of the circle and was one of the most important, basic archetypal patterns in our dreams and fantasies, an "archetype of wholeness." He noted that his patients often created mandalas with the quality of what he called "quaternity"—motifs and designs related to four. Pointing to the use of this symbology in the mandalas made by his patients, he felt that their artworks reflected a "kind of central point within the psyche, to which everything is related, by which everything is arranged, and which is itself a source of energy." Jung felt that dreaming of a four-part mandala represented an unconscious attempt to heal psychic disturbances.

With the straight ruler
I set to work to make
the circle four-cornered.

Aristophanes

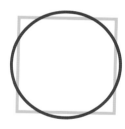

Far left: Squaring the circle is the impossible task of constructing a square with exactly the same area of a given circle, an approximation shown here.

Opposite: Jellyfish display a radial symmetry called tetramerism, a quality of containing four similar parts or sets.

He continues, "The energy of the central point is manifested in the almost irresistible compulsion and urge to become what one is." This urge can also be seen as a desire to dispel the illusion of separation, not only to become what one is, but also to recognize that we are one.

WITH FOUR WE GO 3-D

Adding a fourth point to our mix of dots and lines takes us from Flatland into a world of three-dimensional possibilities. Three points define a two-dimensional shape, but four offer so much more.

Evidence exists that Neolithic people in Scotland conceived of and fashioned spherical stones representing the three-dimensional forms known as the Platonic solids—shapes that were studied extensively by Plato. Beautifully symmetrical in three-dimensional form, with congruent faces, edges, and angles, the five Platonic solids take shape in the unfolding story of substance. As with two-dimensional shapes, the solids offer rich metaphors to describe the continuum of unity's expressions. In his dialogue *Timaeus*, written around 360 BCE, Plato viewed the solids as a representation of the four elements which the ancient people named earth (cube), fire (tetrahedron), water (icosahedron), and air (octahedron)—all of which they saw as surrounding a fifth, more ethereal one that represented the heavens.

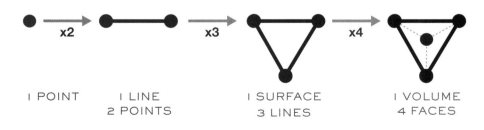

POINT		SURFACE		VOLUME
	LINE	3 LINES		4 FACES
	2 POINTS			

Above, left to right: 3-D progression—1 point; 1 line, 2 points; 1 surface, 3 lines; 1 volume, 4 faces.

Opposite: Tetrahedral-shaped World War II tank obstacles.

Let us assign the cube to earth, for it is the most immobile of the four bodies and most retentive of shape.

Plato

Robert Lawlor states in his book *Sacred Geometry: Philosophy and Practice* (1989), "The Platonist sees our geometrical knowledge as innate in us, having been acquired before birth when our souls were in contact with the realm of ideal being."

Underlying this entire world, from the most dense to the most subtle, there is one substance. This substance is Spirit which has become entranced by the beauty of geometrizing.

Robert Lawlor

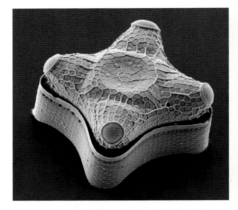

Clockwise from top left: Colored scanning electron micrograph of a diatom; Modern office building; Macro shot of fabric—fibers are woven together, creating a square pattern.

Opposite: Ice cube.

The Platonic Solids

Tetrahedron

Symbol: Fire. The tetrahedron is the first of the Platonic solids. With four sides, it embodies the triangle's inherent strength in that it is the strongest three-dimensional shape and, like the triangle, provides the greatest surface area while enclosing the least volume. In nature, the shape is seen in crystalline forms and joins with the other Platonic solids to create the fundamental structures of all crystals.

Hexahedron

Symbol: Earth. The Platonic solid that embodies four-ness in the shape of a square is the well-known cube. The cube, also known as a hexahedron, brings six squares together to create a stable form that can be seen in crystals such as salt.

Octahedron

Symbol: Air. One of three solids to incorporate the triangle is the octahedron. It appears in the natural world as crystals of diamond, alum, or fluorite.

Icosahedron

Symbol: Water. The icosahedron is composed of twenty triangular faces. The upward pointing tetrahedron can be seen as pointing to the heavens, while downward might be viewed as pointing to the earth. Many viruses have the shape of an icosahedron.

Dodecahedron

Symbol: Heaven. The dodecahedron, with twenty vertices and thirty edges, would be the largest of the Platonic solids if each solid had edges of the same length. Plato referred to the dodecahedron as "quintessence," the fifth element from which the cosmos are made.

TETRAHEDRON

HEXAHEDRON

OCTAHEDRON

ICOSAHEDRON

DODECAHEDRON

Opposite: Fluorite crystal.

Where there is matter,
there is geometry.

Johannes Kepler

Clockwise from top: Bismuth crystals often form intricate, rectangular shapes that display a multicolored iridescence; An ancient mosaic at the Temple of Apollo in Corinth, Greece; Rough octahedral diamond crystal from Kimberley, South Africa.

Opposite: The Kaaba (from the Arabic for "cube," *ka'ba*) is a holy Islamic structure that contains a sacred stone at the Great Mosque in Mecca, Saudi Arabia. Each of its corners points to one of the four points on a compass. Muslims throughout the world face the Kaaba during their daily prayers. During the Hajj pilgrimage, millions of Muslims gather to circle the building on the same day, accomplishing one of the Five Pillars of Islam.

We turn the Cube
and it twists us.

Ernö Rubik

Far left: Rubik's Cube.

Clockwise from top left: Paving stones and lawn squares create an interesting geometric pattern; Spines form a square grid pattern on this prickly pear cactus; Red ixora; A hospital door in Laos displays the symbol of a red cross.

Opposite: The growing habit of this desert succulent creates a four-sided pattern.

We must say that there
are as many squares as
there are numbers.

Galileo Galilei

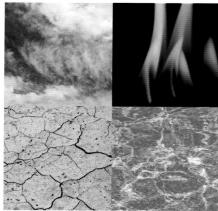

Clockwise from top: The four seasons: spring, summer, autumn, winter; The four cardinal directions: north, south, east, west; The four primary elements: air, fire, earth, water. Some schools of thought include a fifth element known variously as space, idea, void, or ether.

Opposite: *The Quadrad: Mat(t)er*, by P. C. Turczyn, 2009.

PENTAGON

FIVE GROWS ON YOU

From our toes and fingers to the pentagonal shapes of flowers and starfish, five brings a certain spark of life to the world. The solid, material square gets a lift from the addition of a fifth point, which brings with it starry shapes and spiraling ideas. The five elements as described in Tibetan Buddhism are fire, water, air, earth, and a fifth representing space or emptiness. All are interconnected, filling the universe with an amazing array of phenomenon and potential.

The hallmark of five is the pentagon, in which we find stars, spirals, and something especially enigmatic called the "golden ratio." The golden ratio is a mathematical ratio or proportion that is often the growth factor in living forms, which we will examine in "Pentagon: Golden." From spiraling, star-studded galaxies to unfurling ferns, where there's growth, the golden ratio is at work. The fertile pentagon perfectly expresses its qualities of self-reflection and regeneration, for within and without its borders, spirals curl and unfurl as stars find infinite expression.

Pentagons are polygons, meaning "many sided." A regular convex pentagon is composed of five nonintersecting sides of equal length forming equal angles. The three-dimensional representation of the pentagon is the dodecahedron. Having twelve pentagonal faces, the dodecahedron is a Platonic solid that is also known as quintessence, from the Latin *quinta essentia*, meaning "fifth essence."

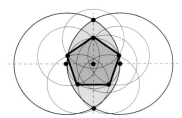

Opposite: Morning glory.

One and one is two,
and two and two is
four, and five will get
you ten if you know
how to work it.

Mae West

FAB FIVES

Pentagons and living forms go together. Some familiar fives that display the nature of the *pentad*, meaning "group of five," are found on our own bodies. There are five appendages to our torso: two arms, two legs, and one head. Each of our arms and legs supports five digits: fingers or toes. Our heads have five openings: two ears, two nostrils, and one mouth; and we have five senses with which we perceive the world: sight, smell, touch, taste, and hearing. The paws and claws of reptiles and mammals also display the quality of five-ness called *pentadactylism*. Even the heads of some animals reflect a pentagonal shape.

Five sounds off in iambic pentameter, the poetic meter of choice for such luminaries as Shakespeare, Milton, and Wordsworth. A favorite harmony is the perfect fifth, and jazz star Paul Desmond put five beats per bar into his famous tune "Take Five."

In religious traditions, five takes on important significance. For Tibetan Buddhists, five plays an essential role in the path to understanding dharma and the Buddha's teachings. The five "Dhyani Buddhas" each symbolize a negative emotional state that, when transformed by practice, can become a positive attribute known as a wisdom. In a mandala, four of the Buddhas are placed at cardinal points with a fifth representing the element of space placed at the center.

Left: The twelve sides of a dodecahedron die are pentagons.

Opposite: Pomegranates cut in half to display five sections. Pomegranates have mythical status in many cultures, sometimes representing fertility and abundance.

To practice five things under all circumstances constitutes perfect virtue; these five are gravity, generosity of soul, sincerity, earnestness, and kindness.

Confucius

The Five Pillars of Islam inform the religious practices of Muslims: *Shahada* (profession of faith), *Salah* (prayers), *Zakat* (giving of alms), *Sawm* (fasting during Ramadan), and *Hajj* (a pilgrimage to Mecca). Numerous Christian traditions hold rituals whose meanings are symbolized in the five wounds of Christ.

WHERE FIVE GOES FROM HERE

Stars and spirals are shapes and patterns emblematic of the pentagon. Both exemplify the regenerative ability of the pentagon and reflect abilities of the golden ratio, a relationship that is aesthetically pleasing for reasons you will see in the sections that follow.

Above, left to right: The Pentagon in Arlington, Virginia, the headquarters of the U.S. Department of Defense, is one of the world's largest office buildings. It has five sides, five floors above ground, and five ring corridors per floor; Pink dianthus; Macro shot of the pentagonal structure of a pineapple skin. The scales on a pineapple tessellate in a pattern that follows the Fibonacci sequence (see page 174).

Left: Sliced okra reveals its pentagonal shape.

Opposite: Antelope horn milkweed has pentagonally shaped buds that open into flowers with five petals.

EXAMPLES OF FIVE-NESS

The pentagonal structure informs the shapes of many natural forms. Pentamerism is a type of radial symmetry in which roughly equal parts are arranged around a central axis equidistant from each other, such as with sea stars and flowers. Variations of the pentagonal shape are also visible in the structure of leaves as well as in the body parts of some animals.

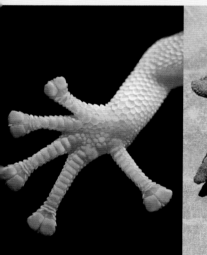

Above, left to right: Foot of a gecko; Leg of an African crocodile; Iguana; Brown bear.

Opposite — top row: Hands of a human adult and child, orchid, maple leaf; **center row:** Dog paw marks in mud, orangutan hand; **bottom row:** Lion, African elephant, horseshoe bat.

GOLDEN

ROOTS OF THE GOLD

Spiraling nautilus shells, whirling hurricanes, and great classical artworks all have something in common. They share a geometric proportion called the golden ratio, or *phi*, that is represented by the symbol Φ. Typically, we think of proportion as a word used to compare the relationship between two sizes or to describe a harmonious balance. In the world of mathematics, proportion refers to the ratio between parts, e.g., 6 is to 3 as 4 is to 2. The golden ratio is a combination of those definitions and is a visually pleasing quality that can be seen in nature as well as in art and architecture.

Neither the pentagonal star nor the spiral could be properly discussed without a brief look into the history of the golden ratio, sometimes called the golden mean or section. The ratio has both geometric and numerical representations. We'll look at a geometric example first.

Ancient peoples referred to the division of one as "golden." Around 300 BCE, Euclid of Alexandria, considered the father of geometry, was said to have given the first definition of the golden ratio as the ratio obtained "when, as the whole line is to the greater segment, so is the greater to the lesser."

Here's how it looks:

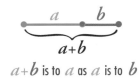

$a+b$ is to a as a is to b

Above: Golden ratio: The whole line $a + b$ is to the greater segment, a, as a is to b. Thus, $(a + b)/a = a/b$. If you set $b=1$ and use a bit of algebra, you find that a equals $(1 + \sqrt{5})/2$, which is the golden ratio.

Opposite: The placement of petals in this dahlia are in the pattern of a golden spiral (see "Pentagon: Spirals," pages 192–209).

The power of the
golden section to create
harmony arises from
its unique capacity to
unite the different parts
of a whole so that
each preserves its own
identity, and yet blends
into the greater pattern
of a single whole.

György Doczi

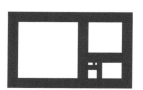

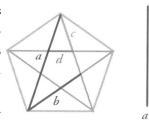

a b c d

Above: Golden proportions are seen
in the arms of this pentagonal star.

Opposite: The proportions of the
golden ratio are demonstrated in the
relationship between the spheres in
this illustration.

Now let's look at how this proportion relates to the pentagon, which has a special relationship with the golden ratio. The diagram to the right is how the ratio looks in a pentagram (from the Greek word *pentagrammon*, meaning "five lines"), the pentagonal star that is inscribed within a pentagon. Note how the proportion between a and b is the same as between b and c. It is also the same proportion as between c and d.

Next, let's look at the numerical properties of *phi*, Φ.

The golden ratio, Φ, has a decimal expansion that never ends and never repeats itself: 1.6180339. . .

It turns out that the golden ratio is the same as another famous number that was derived from a numerical equation that resulted from an imaginary experiment involving the fertility of rabbits.

Fibonacci (Leonardo of Pisa) was an Italian mathematician in the Middle Ages. In his book *Liber abaci* (*The Book of the Abacus*, 1202), Fibonacci discusses a puzzle involving rabbits and the results of their breeding patterns. He posits that the numerical pattern generated by charting the production of rabbit offspring offers a key to the recursive attributes found in nature and geometry. Named for him, the Fibonacci sequence of numbers contains some fascinating characteristics that actually describe how things grow.

Creating the Fibonacci sequence involves some simple math. Really. Even if you're a mathophobe, hang in there—it's easy to understand and well worth it. You'll be amazed at what you'll learn.

Numbers keep recurring
not because we
make them do so
but because they
are inherent in the
proportions of nature
that express the
timeless mathematical
archetypes.

Michael Schneider

FIBONACCI'S PUZZLE

Fibonacci's puzzle employed the use of some very productive rabbits. However, an easier example to understand was developed by a twentieth-century mathematician named Henry Ernest Dudeney. So we'll use his example.

Dudeney favored cows for use in his puzzle, which goes like this: If a cow gives birth to its first she-calf when it is two years old and each offspring gives birth to a she-calf every year after that, how many she-calves are there after twelve years, assuming none die? I'll save you from doing the math on this one. The answer is 144, and here is what each year looks like, starting from year one: 1, 1, 2, 3, 5, 8, 13, 21, 34, 55, 89, 144. This series of numbers is called the Fibonacci sequence and can also be arrived at another way, as we'll see next.

HOW FIBONACCI NUMBERS ADD UP

The first two terms of the Fibonacci sequence are zero and one. The first step is to add them together: 0 + 1 = 1. Then add the last two terms together: 1 + 1 = 2. Next, we add the last two terms: 1 + 2 = 3. The pattern of reproduction continues into infinity and looks like this:

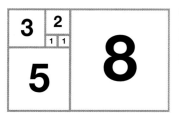

0, 1, 1, 2, 3, 5, 8, 13, 21, 34, 55, and so on. Each figure is the sum of the two numbers that precede it.

Above: The Fibonacci sequence can be used to create golden rectangles. Begin with two squares of the same size. Together they create a rectangle. Continue to add squares with sides that are the length of the longer side of the rectangle (1 + 2 = 3, 2 + 3 = 5, and so on). The longer side of the rectangle will always be a Fibonacci number. If you cut a square off of a golden rectangle, the rectangle that remains is also a golden rectangle.

Opposite: *Time's Golden Arrow*, by Vandorn Hinnant, 2009. These four golden rectangle spirals echo the universal constant; the golden proportion reminds us of its ubiquity throughout nature, as we will see in the coming pages.

The numbers in the Fibonacci sequence increase in size only as a result of building on numbers that already exist in the series. Additional numbers are the result of self-generation; that is, the series grows from within by a process of self-accumulation. And since each term can trace its roots back to zero, each claims an inheritance from the ineffable zero—rather like the fact that all shapes inherit the infinite from their common point.

THE CONNECTION BETWEEN THE GOLDEN RATIO AND FIBONACCI'S SEQUENCE

The ratio that is created by the relationship between adjacent numbers in the Fibonacci sequence gets closer and closer to the golden ratio—the same ratio that is derived from the relationship between the legs of the pentagram. Here's how the ratio is calculated:

Take the ratio of two successive numbers in the sequence (1, 1, 2, 3, 5, 8, 13. . .). In other words, divide any number by the number just before it, and here's what you get:

1/1 = 1; 2/1 = 2; 3/2 = 1.5; 5/3 = 1.666. . . ; 8/5 = 1.6; 13/8 = 1.625; 21/13 = 1.61538 and so on.

While the Fibonacci series ratios never quite exactly match the golden mean, the similarity points to a connection between the two. The link is not hard to see. Remember Euclid's original definition? The line segment is divided into two parts that add up to produce the whole, just like two numbers in Fibonacci's sequence add up to produce the next.

Opposite: Chartres Cathedral, North Rose window. The window's design elements are related to the location of squares that are progressively sized and placed according to golden proportions. According to A. T. Mann, author of *Sacred Architecture* (1993), "The series of squares is an expression of the ultimate organizing geometry, the golden mean." Golden spirals (see "Pentagon: Spiral") expand outward from the center by connecting corners of the squares.

THE FIBONACCI SEQUENCE AND YOU

The pattern made by the string of Fibonacci numbers relates to life in some truly interesting ways. To see an example of the ratio right now, just look at your hands. The lengths of the bones in your hands relate to the ratios in the first four numbers of the Fibonacci sequence.

From your fingertips to your wrist, you'll see the ratio like this: Each bone is larger than the previous one by the ratio of about 1.618. So, if you consider your fingernail the first section, followed by your knuckles and then your hand, all the way down to your wrist, you get the following sequence: 1, 2, 3, 5, 8—all of which are Fibonacci numbers. And it doesn't stop there. The ratio of your forearm to your hand is approximately 1.618. The same holds true for the ratio of your entire arm to your forearm combined with your hand. In fact, your entire body reveals the pattern. Now, this could all be a coincidence (and who knows what reason is behind these interesting similarities), but don't you detect an air of mystery?

> It is stirring to realize that each of the physical structures of the universe is a repackaging of the others. We hold the proportions of the solar system in our hands, face, and whole body.
>
> Michael Schneider

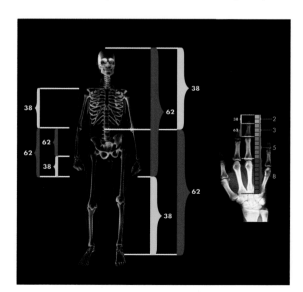

Left: Golden proportions appear throughout the human body. Here, the golden ratio of 1.618 (roughly 62:38) is seen in a variety of measurements in the body. We can also see the golden proportions revealed by the Fibonacci sequence as it relates to the bone structure of our hands.

Opposite: *Vitruvian Man*, by Leonardo da Vinci, ca. 1490. The drawing is based on the relationship between ideal human proportions and geometry, as discussed by the ancient Roman architect Vitruvius (after whom the drawing is named) in his treatise *De architectura*, ca. 25 BCE.

The discovery of the innate meaning of numbers is therefore a primary creative legacy of sacred architecture.

A. T. Mann

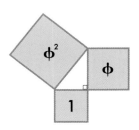

You see these very proportions throughout nature. The pinecone offers yet another example. In most cones, the degree of variation in the location of each scale contributes to the creation of a spiral. The pattern created is the most efficient way to pack as many seeds as possible into an area without crowding. Similar spiraling structures reflecting the golden mean can be seen in sunflowers and other plants, as well as mollusk shells such as the nautilus. For more about spirals, see "Pentagon: Spirals."

You'll also see the golden mean represented in art and architecture. Its visual appeal is revealed in many ancient Greek buildings, such as the Parthenon in Athens, where detailing from large to small utilizes the proportions. Leonardo da Vinci's classic painting *Mona Lisa* employs the golden rectangle to define the space in which the model's face appears. The golden mean is appealing to us because it exemplifies the organic proportional balance inherent throughout nature.

KEPLER'S "PRECIOUS JEWEL"

German mathematician and astronomer Johannes Kepler (1571–1630) was a big fan of the golden ratio, calling it a "precious jewel." He said, "Geometry has two great treasures: one is the Theorem of Pythagoras, and the other the division of a line into extreme and mean ratio [i.e. golden ratio]; the first we may compare to a measure of gold, the second we may name a precious jewel." He combined the two treasures to create the Kepler triangle, a right triangle that is created by three squares whose areas relate to the golden ratio. Kepler was also famous for recognizing the regular star polyhedra (see next chapter).

Left: The Kepler triangle is a right triangle formed by the edges of three squares that progress in size according to the golden ratio.

Opposite: The golden rectangle overlaid on the visage of Leonardo da Vinci's *Mona Lisa*, ca. 1519.

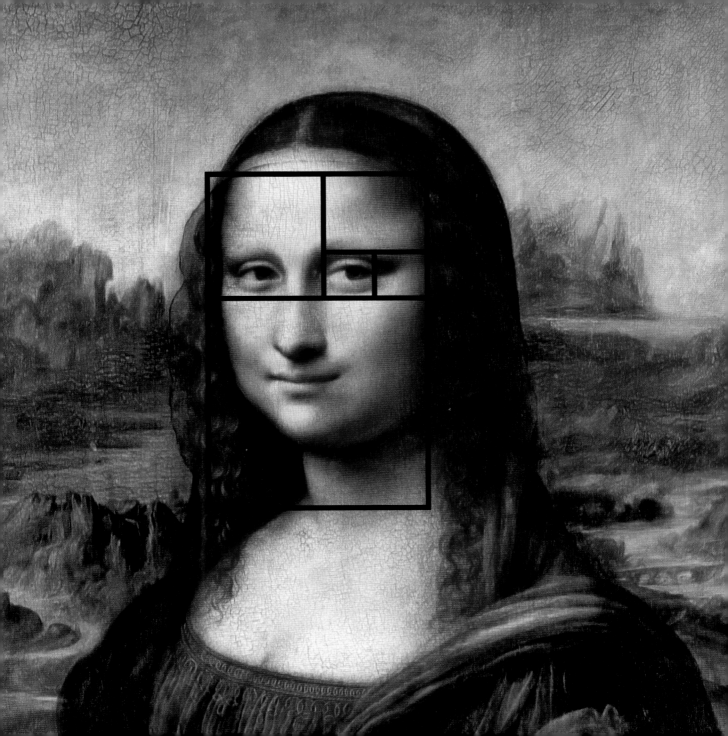

Stars

STARSTRUCK

Stars have an illustrious place in history, making their appearance here and there as symbols of excellence and protection. Star symbols have been found on shards of pots in Palestine that date back as far as 4000 BCE and are believed to have been used by Sumerians around 2700 BCE as a symbol for heaven and the four corners of the earth.

Pythagoreans (the followers of Pythagoras) were drawn to the mathematical perfection of the pentagon and associated the pentagram with Hygeia, the mythological Greek goddess of health. The star was used as a sacred emblem of their secret society, a badge by which they could recognize one another. Believing that information about the pentagram should be guarded, the Pythagoreans prevented distribution of the pentagram's construction in written word. For a thousand years, knowledge about the pentagram was kept under cover, not appearing in any written texts until Luca Pacioli (Leonardo da Vinci's math teacher) introduced it to the public in 1509 in his book, *De divina proportione*.

Left: Star-shaped elderberry flowers.

Opposite: Sacred datura.

WHOLE PARTS

The stars come out when the pentagon displays its ability to regenerate. With five sides and five angles, the pentagon is the natural nesting place for a pentagram, which in turn makes a nice place to nestle another, and another—all parts of the whole (see illustrations below). This quality of self-similarity is infinitely expressed in both inward and outward directions, relating it to the iterative quality of fractals, a fascinating subject we will explore in Chapter 7, "Patterns: Fractals."

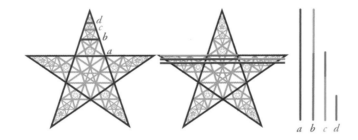

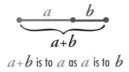

$a+b$ is to a as a is to b

Top, left to right: Pentagrams are packed with gold, as can be seen in a variety of ways. In the first pentagram, successively smaller stars inscribed in the arm of the parent star create sections whose widest width, when compared with one another, is related to the golden ratio. In the second pentagram, lines are drawn between segments of the star to reveal yet more golden relationships. In both examples, compare the relationships between the lines and you'll see the golden ratio, or Φ. The vertical colored lines illustrate how all the lines "add up" to create golden relationships.

Center: The whole line, $a + b$, is to the greater segment, a, as a is to b. Thus, $(a + b)/a = a/b$. These same ratios are seen in the preceding pentagram diagrams.

Bottom: As we saw on page 178, the Φ relationship is literally in our bones. Here the entire body reflects the starry pattern of the "divine proportion," as it was called by the Italian mathematician Luca Pacioli in *De divina proportione* (1509).

Opposite: Cross section of a star fruit.

Keep your eyes on
the stars, and your
feet on the ground.

Theodore Roosevelt

SPIRALING CONNECTIONS

By utilizing a replicative technique related to the golden mean, the geometric ratio created by the Fibonacci sequence, the arms of the star serve as wombs for the growing golden spiral (see "Pentagon: Spirals," page 198).

STARRING ROLES

The apple provides a stellar example of the pentagram's shape echoed from blossom to fruit. Besides being present in the five-petal blossom of the apple tree, the star pattern is mimicked in the indentations on the bottom of the fruit as well as in the seed pattern when the apple is cut in half. This feature can also be seen in the blossoms of other edible fruits and vegetables.

The trait of self-replication plays out in nongeometric ways as well. A familiar example is the starfish's ability to regenerate by fragmentation; if it has the misfortune of losing a leg, it just grows another one, and the lost leg can even grow itself a new body.

Left and opposite: Both the seeds of an apple and the blossom on the tree display pentagrams, as seem in this cross section of an apple, and this apple tree blossom.

Begin doing what
you want to do now.
We are not living in
eternity. We have only
this moment, sparkling
like a star in our
hand—and melting like
a snowflake.

Sir Francis Bacon

From the period between 300 and 150 BCE, the city of Jerusalem employed the pentagram as its official seal, predating the use of the six-pointed star presently associated with Jewish culture.

During the Middle Ages, the beautiful star took a sad turn: When inverted with a single point at the bottom, it was thought to represent magic and the devil. Yet Nordic countries posted them (point up) on their barns to ward off trolls and evil spirits.

The pentagram has a starring role in literature and shone brightly in a fourteenth-century story called *Sir Gawain and the Green Night* (author unknown). The pentagram appears as an important symbol on Gawain's shield, representing, among other things, five virtues: generosity, fellowship, chastity, courtesy, and compassion.

Above: Cactus shaped like a star.

Opposite—top row: A *drudenfuss*, or magical symbol intended to ward off *drudes* (malevolent, possessed virgins and priestesses), on a house in Ahrweiler, Germany, from 1639; Starflower; **center row:** Star with the word *freedom* under it, carved into stone in an unknown location in Wyoming, Five sepals of a tomato, *Hoya Carnosa*; **bottom row:** Sand dollar, Morning glory.

When it is darkest,
men see the stars.

Ralph Waldo Emerson

As the official symbol of the Bahá'í faith, the pentagram is called *haykal*, which is Arabic for "temple." Taoists utilized the star encased within a circle (a pentacle) to represent fire, earth, metal, water, and wood.

Stars make an excellent gift. Entertainers can tell you that getting a star set in pavement on Hollywood Boulevard is a very good thing. Any child knows that getting a gold star means "great job." And a fifth star on your military uniform signifies your seniority within the ranks.

In the natural world, the star pattern is a thing of beauty. From five-petal flowers to starfish, pentagrams will always delight the eye of the beholder.

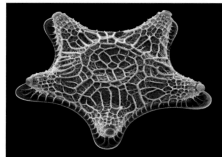

Right from top to bottom: Flag of the European Union; Frangipani, used to make leis on many Pacific islands; Underside of a starfish—its pentagonal mouth is at the center; Colored scanning electron micrograph of a diatom.

Opposite—top row: Cross section of a papaya fruit, red starfish on top of coral; **center row:** Red star on top of the famous Spasskaya tower of the Kremlin in Moscow, spreading bellflower, cluster of scarlet milkweed; **bottom row:** Godzilla's star on the Hollywood Walk of Fame in Los Angeles, Texas Ranger badge.

Spirals

SPIRALING INTO SPACE

Our lives are spiraling around us—generating and regenerating, expanding and contracting, pushing out and pulling in. Some days we might feel as if we're on the forefront of a life whorling out of control. At other times we might feel we're slipping into the calm center of a peaceful spiral. The spiral coils into and out of infinity, constantly changing and exchanging energy.

Circles go round and round, but spirals suggest progression and growth, reaching continuously outward from the center. Symbolizing regeneration, renewal, and rebirth, spirals have been observed in the nature of growth as well as in the growth of nature. The self-replicative trait of spirals can also be observed in the stunning imagery of fractals, where the whole is in the parts and the parts are in the whole. Fractals are created by a recursive equation that folds back into itself, resulting in images that offer a taste of the cosmos as well as a window into the patterns of natural forms (see "Patterns: Fractals"). This recursive trait can be found in the Fibonacci sequence as well (see "Pentagon: Golden").

While our lives may resemble hurricanes twisting and turning around us in a stormy display, if we look closely we can find a center of stillness—the eye and "I" of our personal mandala—the zero point from which all things spin and spring. Accessing that place of calm requires quieting the distracting noise of life, an endeavor that often involves the acts of meditation and contemplation.

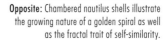

Opposite: Chambered nautilus shells illustrate the growing nature of a golden spiral as well as the fractal trait of self-similarity.

Growth is a spiral
process, doubling back
on itself, reassessing
and regrouping.

Julia Margaret Cameron

Spirals can be seen as metaphors for personal growth and may take form in tools for self-reflection. One such tool is the labyrinth, a spiraling path that has long been used as an instrument to draw oneself into meditation by following its route to the center. Unlike a maze that is designed to confuse, the labyrinth offers only one way into and one way out of its center, and can be used to quietly explore one's inner psyche.

The spiral's two-way trait of inward and outward movement might be viewed metaphorically as the road we take to find our own truth. For some, it can be a journey of self-awareness, searching for meaning by looking inward. Others approach their paths as a pilgrimage or hero's journey, as with Percival's search for the Holy Grail. Yet other paths leading to one's center may include outward expressions and explorations in the arts, sciences, or mathematics. All are journeys that take the traveler to a central destination that may also serve as a starting point for another adventure.

Left: Computer-generated
illustration of a spiral galaxy.

Opposite: A low-pressure
system swirling off the
southwestern coast of Iceland.

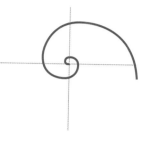

ONE CENTER, TWO SPIRALS

All spirals pivot around a fixed point, though they can grow outward in different ways. Archimedean spirals expand from a central point at a constant rate, as seen in the shape of a coiled rope or spiderweb, or in the tightly nested grooves on a vinyl record.

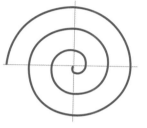

The spiral that appears most frequently in nature is the golden spiral. While it finds kinship with the Archimedean spiral in that they both begin with the infinite point, the golden spiral increases the distance between coils as it grows. This spiral comes alive within the shape of a pentagonal star, another symbol of regeneration. The regenerative properties of the star (see page 184) are a reflection of its curvaceous counterpart, the golden spiral. The pattern of its growth and expansion is utilized by nature in the creation of shells, animal horns, tornados, and galaxies. From the uncurling of a leaf to stars spinning in space, golden spirals are indicators that growth is taking place.

This seems to be the law of progress in everything we do; it moves along a spiral rather than a perpendicular; we seem to be actually going out of the way, and yet it turns out that we were really moving upward all the time.

Frances E. Willard

Above from top: Golden spiral; Archimedean spiral; The Archimedean spiral of a coiled rope.

Opposite: The frond of a fern unfurls in a golden spiral.

GROWING GOLD

The golden spiral is formed by the self-replicating pattern of the golden ratio. From the swirling paths of elementary particles in a bubble chamber to galaxies spinning around in the heavens, golden spirals leave their mark on the universe in many ways.

Every daisy and sunflower is a window on the infinite.

György Doczi

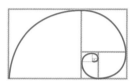

Golden spirals can be made from both golden rectangles and golden triangles, each of which embodies the mystifying numerical relationship of phi. Golden triangles are found in pentagons and make up the "arms" of pentagonal stars.

By connecting certain vertices in either the golden rectangle or star, a logarithmic or equiangular spiral is made. Such a spiral does not change its shape as it increases in size, a trait that is referred to as self-similarity. The golden spiral can be used as a template to observe the nature of the infinite displayed in the finite. The growth pattern reflecting the golden spiral provides an efficient way to space out growth. The seed pattern on a sunflower, the spiraling bracts of a pinecone, and even the number of petals on a flower offer views of the golden spiral, as well as the Fibonacci sequence, in action.

Above, from top: Golden spirals find room to expand in the golden rectangle. See "Pentagon: Stars" for an example of the golden spiral's relationship with pentagrams; By utilizing a replicative technique related to the golden mean (the geometric ratio created by the Fibonacci sequence), the arms of the star serve as wombs for the growing golden spiral.

Left: The yellow lines on this pinecone illustrate just one of the two opposing spirals created by the positioning of the bract scales.

Opposite: The placement of seeds in a sunflower mirror the same double spiral pattern found in the pinecone as well as other plants. See page 171 for a similar example found in the dahlia.

The growth of
understanding follows
an ascending spiral
rather than a
straight line.

Joanna Field

HELICES

The helix is not necessarily a spiral, though the two are often confused. According to the *American Heritage Science Dictionary*, a helix is "a curve turning about an axis on the surface of a cylinder or cone while rising at a constant upward angle from a base."

When rotation is combined with the spiral curve of a helix, you get a screw. There are two kinds of helices—left-handed and right-handed. They may look similar, but just try opening a bottle of wine with a corkscrew by turning it counterclockwise. You'll find it a counterproductive activity. Helices also find expression in the helical structure of spiral bindings, staircases, and corkscrew pasta. Examples from nature include the DNA double helix and certain bacteria.

Above, left to right: Energy-saving compact fluorescent light bulb; Screw; Rotini pasta; Computer-generated 3-D rendering of a strand of DNA; Corkscrew opening a wine bottle.

Opposite: This seashell displays a conical helix.

The spiral tendency within each one of us is the longing for and growth towards wholeness.

Jill Purce

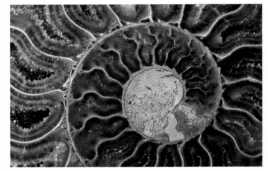

Clockwise from top left: Snail on a dew-covered blade of grass; Spiral decoration on an old rusted iron gate; Spiral petroglyph carved onto a rock surface by prehistoric Anasazi Native Americans in Utah; Crinoid, also known as a sea lily or featherstar. Crinoids use their featherlike arms to filter small particles of food from the sea water; Detail of an ammonite fossil from the Jurassic Period.

Opposite: Curled-up millipede on green moss.

The spiral mandala shows the path through the universe, concentrating not on static perfection but on the equilibrium of its essential flow.

Jill Purce

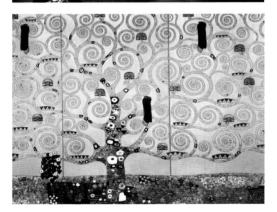

The graceful curve of a spiral is a popular architectural and artistic design element.

Top left: Tulip staircase and glass roof lantern, as seen from below, in the Queen's House in Greenwich, England, built between 1614–17. This staircase is particularly significant as it was the first centrally unsupported staircase constructed in England.

Center left: Spiral-shaped stained glass Glory Window of Thanksgiving Chapel, in Thanks-Giving Square, Dallas, Texas.

Bottom left: Detail of a design for *Tree of Life*, ca. 1909, by Austrian Symbolist artist Gustav Klimt. Spirals are a recurring element in Klimt's art.

Above: Romanesque door of the parish church in Pürgg, Styria, Austria. The spirals are believed to defend the church against *böser Geister*, or evil spirits.

Opposite: Microscopic shot of compound crystals from the semiconductor alloy indium antimonide.

The human mind
always makes progress,
but it is a progress
in spirals.

Madame de Staël

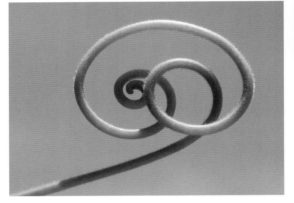

Left from top: Close-up of the leaves of a spiral aloe in southern Africa; Tendril of a purple passionflower plant; Sheep with large spiral horns.

Above: Macro shot of a green tulip bud.

Opposite: Colored photograph showing tracks left by subatomic particles from a particle accelerator at CERN, the European particle physics laboratory in Geneva, Switzerland. Atomic particles, forced to accelerate at extremely high speeds in a particle accelerator, leave spiraling paths of tiny bubbles as they move through a liquid-filled bubble chamber.

Love and hatred,
ignorance and wisdom
find balance in the
spiral dance of life.

Michael Schneider

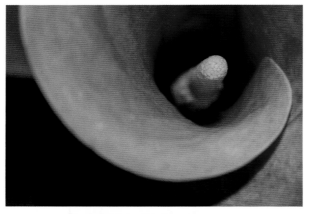

Left from top: The tail of a tropical
chameleon curled into a spiral;
Macro shot of an orange calla lily;
Detail of a violin handle.

Opposite: The arm of an octopus.

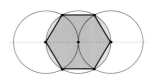

HEXAGON

SIX PACKED

The hexagon comes with six sides ready to hook up and get organized. This structure allows the hexagon to function in an orderly way—an attribute that works efficiently in situations when close packing is necessary. As with triangles and squares, hexagons fit together snugly and lend themselves to *tessellating*, a quality of tiling that completely fills a plane, with no gaps or overlaps. This trait comes in handy for repeated patterns, such as those found in floors, wallpaper, and, of course, beehives.

Ancient peoples called six a "perfect" number because of its special property of being the sum of all its divisors (1 + 2 + 3 = 6). The hexagon, as a symbol of six, enjoys a connection with the triangle—two of which, when overlapped, create a hexagonal star, or *hexagram*. The numerical connection is obvious: 3 + 3 = 6. With six sides of equal length, a regular hexagon has sixfold rotational symmetry and sixfold reflection symmetry.

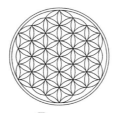

Left: The Flower of Life is a sacred geometric pattern that consists of circles overlapping to form a flowerlike, hexagonal symmetry. A derivative of the Flower of Life pattern, called the Fruit of Life, is drawn with lines connecting the center points of each circle. From this template, one can create a design called Metatron's Cube (**below, left**). Projections of the Platonic solids (see page 154)—tetrahedron, hexahedron (cube), octahedron, dodecahedron, icosahedron—can be drawn within the cube, lending a special significance to the design for geometers.

Metatron's Cube　　Tetrahedron　　Hexahedron (cube)　　Octahedron　　Dodecahedron　　Icosahedron

Opposite: Microscopic shot of phosphotungstic acid crystallized in the form of a dodecahedron, which creates a hexagonal silhouette viewed head-on.

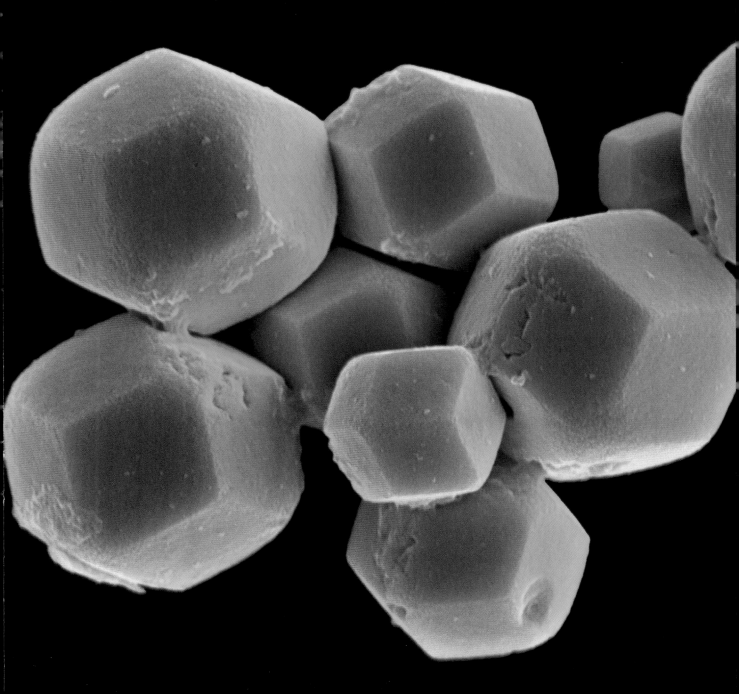

HEX APPEAL

Wherever hexagons are found, you can be sure to also find a need for a streamlined structure. Hexagonal configurations created by three-way junctions at 120-degree angles "allow nature to accomplish the most with the least," according to Pat Murphy in her book, *By Nature's Design* (1993). The complex, compound eyes of bees contain over 7,000 hexagonal facets. Each is oriented in a different direction, enabling a broad range of vision and the ability to detect small shifts in movement. It is interesting to note that the efficient hexagonal structure of bee eyes is also employed in their nests, which benefit from the functionality of the honeycomb construction design as it requires a minimal amount of wax and offers a sturdy container for honey storage. A hexagonally ordered collection of closely packed kernels also appears in the arrangement of corn on the cob—all the better to get maximum input when biting a mouthful. Tortoise shells and snakeskins both employ the close-packing hexagon in the creation of their outer layers.

That which is not good for the bee-hive cannot be good for the bees.

Marcus Aurelius

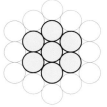

Clockwise from top left: Close packing of corn kernels creates a hexagonal pattern; Six same-size circles arrayed around a center circle so they all "kiss" each other (touching without overlapping) make a hexagonal flowerlike design that is an efficient stacking method for bottles, barrels, and other cylindrical structures; Empty wine bottles are stored in compartments and rows that employ hexagons for easy stacking.

Opposite: The hexagonal structure of a honeycomb provides efficient storage for honey and for maturing larvae.

Who carved the
nucleus, before it fell,
into six horns of ice?

Johannes Kepler

Another variation on the six-around-one theme is illustrated when circles cluster and compete for space. The stretchy, translucent film of soap and water offers a view into the world of H_2O molecules trying their best to minimize the bubble's surface area. When the water molecule's urge to merge with its mates is balanced with the simultaneous outward push of air, hexagonal shapes are created that form 120-degree joints.

While hexagonal patterns do appear in living, organic nature, they are more commonly found in inanimate natural forms, most notably in snowflakes. Some appear as simple hexagons; however, the ones in which we usually delight are star shaped and delicately intricate. Snowflakes take shape from the hexagonal lattice formed by the water molecules of an ice crystal. As they grow, the crystals sprout branches from their corners that can develop into feathery and lacy designs or faceting that is less ornate. Changes in temperature and humidity affect how crystals grow, giving snowflakes their diverse, individualized appearance.

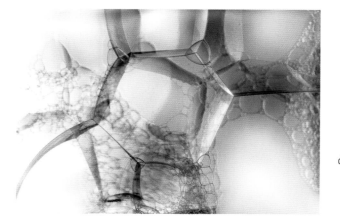

Left: Macro shot of soap bubbles, displaying their hexagonal formation.

Opposite: Microscopic images of snowflakes reveal an intricate, hexagonal structure.

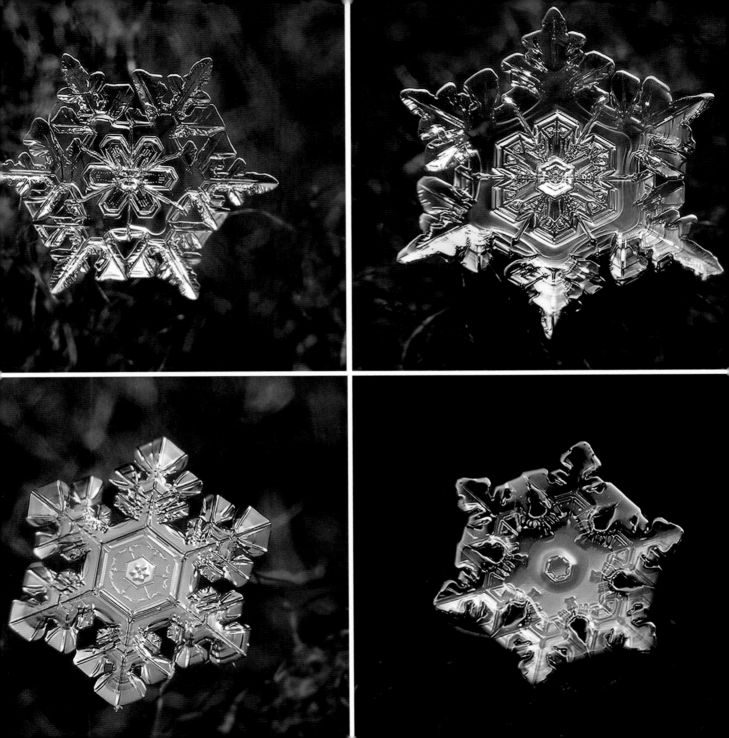

THE CULTURAL PERSPECTIVE

Though most commonly associated with Judaism nowadays, the hexagram has a rich history as a symbol found in many cultures and religions. The earliest examples of the hexagram, or hexagonal star, are dated between 800 to 600 BCE. In the early Middle Ages, the hexagram was associated with magic, though it was also used as an ornamental element by Christians and Muslims in architecture and artwork.

During the seventeenth century, the hexagram was used to represent the chemical science of alchemy, symbolizing harmony between the opposing elements of fire and water. During the same period, the symbol is also said to have become associated with the mystical branch of Judaism known as Kabbalah. The desire to adopt a potent symbol to represent Judaism in the nineteenth century led to the selection of the hexagram—also known as the *Magen David*, or "Shield of David"—which now appears on the national flag of Israel.

> The laws of nature are but the mathematical thoughts of God.
>
> Euclid

Left to right: A fragment of an ancient Roman mosaic, dating from the beginning of the third century CE, at El Djem Museum in Tunisia; Hexagonal and triangular tiles fit together to form a hexagram. The tiles are from the Topkapi Palace, Istanbul, Turkey. Completed ca. 1473, the palace was the imperial residence of the Ottoman sultans for almost four hundred years.

Opposite: A stained-glass window in a synagogue features the Magen David, or Star of David.

Every flower is a soul
blossoming in nature.

Gérard de Nerval

This shape is also found in Hindu and Buddhist mandalas. In the Hindu Tantric tradition, hexagrams appear in the design of *yantras* (mystical diagrams used for meditation). An inverted triangle represents the female and a triangle pointed upward symbolizes the male. When these two shapes are brought together to form a hexagram, they represent, as Madhu Khanna states in her book *Yantra* (1973), "the concept of the fusion of polarities, the male and female, spirit and matter, the static and the kinetic in a perfect state of unity."

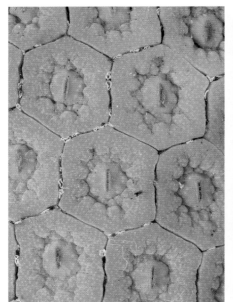 

Above, left to right: A macro shot of the inflorescence of an unknown plant shows hexagonal stacking; The honeycomb grouper is so named because of the hexagonal honeycomb pattern of its skin.

Opposite: Tiger lily in a garden, with its reflection in water. Most lilies have six petals.

Art is the imposing of a
pattern on experience,
and our aesthetic
enjoyment is recognition
of the pattern.

Alfred North Whitehead

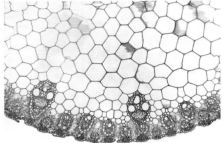

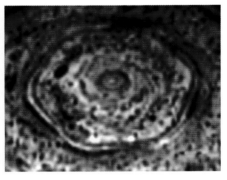

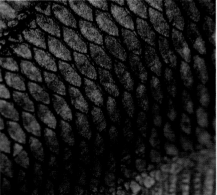

Clockwise from top left: Hexagonal nuts stack
nicely; Magnified cross section of sugar cane.
As with bubbles, the tension between cell walls
creates hexagonal shapes; Scientists have noted an
interesting similarity in shapes between the polygons
created by rotating fluids in laboratories and this
hexagonal-shaped cloud feature on Saturn; Macro
shot of the scales of a Siamese fighting fish.

Opposite: Light microscopic image of a diatom.

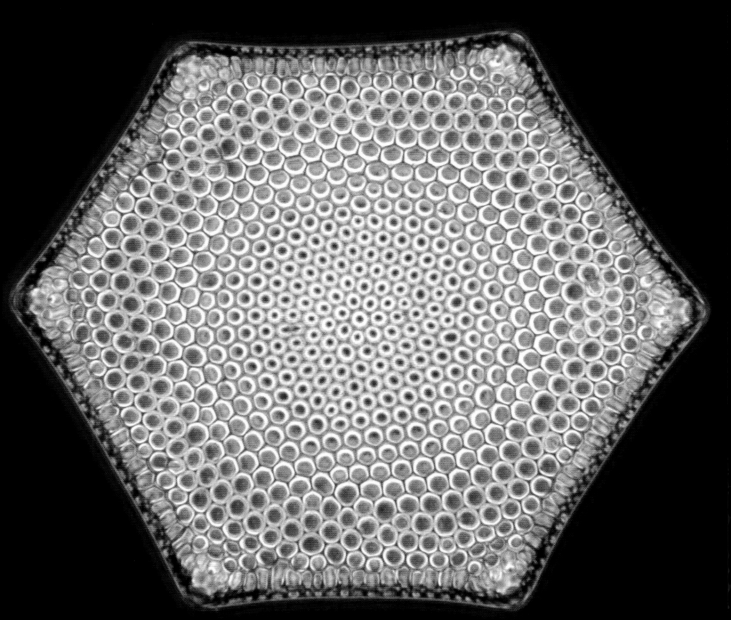

Geometry enlightens
the intellect and sets
one's mind right.

Ibn Khaldun

Above: Star sapphire cabochon. A star sapphire is a type of sapphire that exhibits asterism, an optical phenomenon in which an enhanced reflective area appears in the shape of a star on the surface of a cabochon (a smooth, unfaceted gemstone) cut from the stone. Star sapphires derive their six-rayed asterism from titanium dioxide impurities.

Left: Hippeastrum. All Hippeastrum flowers have six tepals: three outer sepals and three inner petals.

Opposite: Giant's Causeway in County Antrim, Northern Ireland. Some fifty to sixty million years ago, volcanic activity caused highly fluid molten basalt to intrude through chalk beds, forming an extensive lava plateau. The fracture network caused by the cooling lava produced the distinctive columns seen today, most of which are hexagonal.

Patterns

PATTERN RECOGNITION

A mandala can be as simple as a circle or as complex as the web of a spider. Each example illustrates a pattern. In the case of the spiderweb, a fragment can be viewed separate from the entire web, yet, it is still a part of a whole. Indeed, we can even study the part to help us understand the whole. So it is with the patterns described in this chapter. While they do not necessarily appear mandalic in nature, they do indeed illustrate aspects of the whole of the mandala.

Case in point: One beautiful spring morning during a hike, a friend and I observed my dog Sasha crouching behind a tree as if to hide herself. Though her girth was clearly visible on either side of the tree, we realized that she was indeed hiding when she surprised my friend's dog with a gleeful pounce, like a three-year-old child yelling "Boo!" to scare her mother. My friend and I mused on Sasha's prank, not realizing that it was the first of many surprise attacks to come. It was on her third reenactment that we began to see a pattern develop. To this day, five years later, Sasha continues to delight us with encore performances.

Pattern observation involves more than you might think. While it may amuse and entertain, it also offers an opportunity to look more deeply into many areas of study, including those involving the weightier questions of life. Pattern is a combination of traits, tendencies, or qualities that form a consistent arrangement that then characterizes an individual or group. Life abounds with patterns as well as disciplines with which to study them. In science, the process of pattern recognition involves the classification of objects into categories or classes.

Opposite: A male peacock displays
the iterative pattern of its plumes.

All are but parts of one
stupendous whole,
whose body Nature is,
and God the soul.

Alexander Pope

Mathematics has been described as the science of pattern, while behavioral patterns are the focus of psychological studies. Artists delight in using pattern to adorn and embellish, and musicians utilize patterns of notes to create melodies.

Closely related to the notion of archetype, patterns are found in many different fields, from business to science to art, providing a structure or model that supplies order or common attributes to the things or people that participate in a group.

In Jungian psychology, an archetype is a universal pattern of thought/belief or symbolic imagery that informs behavior, consciously or unconsciously. Based on themes brought forward from past collective experience, an archetypal image (or unconscious role model) may be present in one's unconscious, asserting that if you behave in a certain way, you will find success or fulfillment in a particular role.

The archetypal image of a hero appears in many cultures, manifesting in ours as Superman (or Supermom). Sometimes a therapist needs to tease out the archetypal image in order to shed light on it, thereby helping a patient to grapple with issues that might stem from unconscious yet cherished beliefs.

For example, a man or woman harboring a superhero archetypal image/role model may fight for truth or justice by involving him or herself in first one cause, then another, and then another—sometimes to the detriment of not only each cause, but also their personal health and well-being and their relationships with those around them. Recognizing the influence of the archetypal

Opposite: Curled ball python. The pattern of scales covering a snake's skin can give important clues as to whether your safety is at stake—if you know what to look for.

pattern may free the person to choose whether or not to take a more moderate approach toward fulfilling his or her need to champion a cause. In this way, "need" can be transformed into simple "desire" and "to champion" can be replaced by "to serve"—still heroic, perhaps, but minus the impossible dream of being more superhuman than human.

PATTERNS PAST AND PRESENT

Pattern has been an object of study since ancient times. In the sixth century BCE, Greek philosophers pondered such meaningful questions as "What is reality made of?" The Pythagoreans directed their inquiry toward the study of form and pattern rather than strictly physical substance. Aristotle developed a system of thought involving a unified approach to the exploration of both form and substance that prevailed for two thousand years.

The Scientific Revolution of the sixteenth and seventeenth centuries spawned the creation of modern science. Discoveries in the natural world were accompanied by a mechanistic worldview, in which an analytic approach to the study of phenomena was restricted to observing pieces of a complex unit in order to understand it as a whole.

The Romantic movement that began in the late eighteenth century offered a return to the more all-embracing philosophy of Aristotle. In opposition to the mechanistic approach to examination of phenomena, poets and philosophers such as Johann Wolfgang von Goethe and Immanuel Kant proposed a more dynamic and all-inclusive approach to life study. As Goethe wrote, "Each creature is but a patterned gradation of one great harmonious whole." The move toward a more holistic view was not smooth, yet in the early twentieth century a paradigm shift in systems thinking began to take hold.

Opposite: Computer-generated illustration.

From the systems point of view, the understanding of life begins with the understanding of pattern.

Fritjof Capra

WHOLE RELATIONSHIPS

The advent of quantum theory in the 1920s caused the study of particles (parts) to take an amazing turn. No longer was the particle seen as a lonely entity in a sea of unrelated events and substance. It was in relationship with itself and everything else. As American physicist Henry Stapp observed, "An elementary particle is not an independently existing unanalyzable entity. It is, in essence, a set of relationships that reach outward to other things." These relationships are considered probabilities whose behavior is determined by an entire system.

In classical physics, parts were considered to be wholly independent, self-contained entities. Quantum physics turned this notion upside down when it asserted that the parts cannot be understood without acknowledging their relationship to the whole, and vice versa. It was observed that infinite parts were acting in concert with, not independent of, a system that informed the way things work. Suddenly the news was out that things might not be what they seem.

Investigations into the subatomic world have led to the creation of a holistic worldview that considers systems to be integrated wholes rather than merely a collection of parts. Pattern study eventually became acknowledged as critical to developing an understanding of life systems, and, in the 1930s, a new way of thinking about systems was developed by biologists, psychologists, and ecologists. There was a return to regarding Earth itself as an integrated whole, as it had been previously viewed in pre-Hellenic Greece and even earlier. The mandala pattern of connected elements evolving from, and revolving around, a unifying center began to regain its place of importance in the scientific worldview.

Opposite: Beech forest in springtime. The tree, with its trunk, branches, and roots, provides a symbol for seeing the earth as an integrated whole—a mandala composed of elements connected by a unifying symbol.

The web, then, or
the pattern, a web
at once sensuous and
logical, an elegant
and pregnant texture:
that is style, that is the
foundation of the art
of literature.

Robert Louis Stevenson

During World War II, a new intellectual movement was born that focused on observing patterns of communication, especially in networks. From this movement sprang a new science called cybernetics, a term invented by American mathematician Norbert Wiener. Cybernetics involves the study of system structures utilizing a mechanism called feedback, a signal that informs the system of a change in the environment caused by phenomena. The signal allows the system to change behavior to adapt to a new condition.

For example, a child learns to walk as a result of constant feedback from her body's nerves telling her that certain moves work or don't work. This concept applies to smaller and larger networks. On a larger scale, feedback given to city representatives by community members may reveal that certain laws do not benefit their constituents and require legislative adjustment. Feedback is recognized as a way for life forms to balance themselves through a process of self-regulation.

The study of ideas relating to self-organization in cybernetics has expanded since its conception. It eventually progressed into a more enlarged view in which the world was seen as a "web of life," a concept that was perfectly described by Longchenpa as: an "integrated structure organized around a unifying center."

Opposite: A beautiful Buddhist metaphor called "Indra's Net" employs the image of a web to illustrate the interconnectedness of all things. The web is imagined as a multidimensional net, covered with jewel-like dewdrops. Each drop reflects the other drops to create an infinite, sparkling example of a holographic universe, wherein each part contains information relating to all the other parts.

We are but whirlpools in a river of ever-flowing water. We are not stuff that abides, but patterns that perpetuate themselves.

Norbert Wiener

The study of life systems now involves a coordinated process utilizing two scientific methods of studying life-form patterns: the study of structure, or quantifying, an approach requiring the weighing and measuring of things; and form study and pattern mapping, known as qualifying. While both methods are important, it is the second approach of pattern study that enlivens the first.

Austrian-American physicist Fritjof Capra states in *The Web of Life* (1997), "While it is true that all living organisms are ultimately made of atoms and molecules, they are not 'nothing but' atoms and molecules. There is something else to life, something nonmaterial and irreducible—a pattern of organization." An amazing feature of pattern is that it can take us into and out of deep and infinitely expansive realms, none of which is solid or fixed. (This feature is not unlike that found in fractals; see "Patterns: Fractals.")

When we examine the structure of atoms with a microscope, we find that they exhibit patterns created by the electrons, protons, and neutrons of which the atoms are comprised—all participating in a constant whirl of activity in which no part remains in the same place. Decreasing the magnification of our microscopes, we can see the patterns of increasingly larger organizations of DNA, cells, organs, and on up to a whole human being—patterns on patterns that can all be traced back to that original point, where we find nothing but the infinite. As we continue to enlarge on this view, we see that even our bodies do not have boundaries that would separate, or isolate, the inside from the out. Our bodies are parts of larger systems of patterns that extend into what we now term "the infinite."

Opposite: Macro shot of a red geranium leaf.

In examining the structure of our lives, the environment, and indeed the entire world in which we live, we must also be aware of the patterns we generate and determine whether they contribute to a salubrious climate in which to live as individuals and a community. Any way you look at it, life appears to be an organized affair comprised of interdependent players, all working together to create an amazing universe.

SYMMETRY

The study of patterns involves the examination of symmetry, of which American mathematician Thomas J. McFarlane states, "Symmetry is the archetypal key that unlocks the true nature of the world." He goes further: "In this world of apparent diversity, symmetry is both the link to our origin and the key to our destiny, connecting diversity with unity on every level."

While the word *symmetry* most commonly brings to mind images of balance and equal proportion, its study becomes much more intricate in mathematics. A variety of symmetry types are associated with different transformations, such as rotation, reflection, and scaling. The type we most easily recognize is called bilateral symmetry, which is simple right–left reflection symmetry. Familiar examples of this symmetry are found in the bodies of humans, giraffes, butterflies, and centipedes. Each entity sports a recognizable right–left symmetry.

Rotational symmetry has a spin quality in which the object displays symmetry by rotating around a center point. Starfish offer a good example of this, as do inanimate objects such as snowflakes. Of course, these examples can also display bilateral symmetry, as the trait of symmetry is not necessarily limited to one expression per object.

Opposite: Bilateral symmetry is beautifully apparent in butterflies.

Our biggest failure
is our failure to
see patterns.

Marilyn Ferguson

In biology, closer inspection reveals that symmetry is only approximate. The left side of your body is not perfectly symmetrical to the right—perhaps because of a crooked smile inherited from Great-Aunt Erma or a close call with a cat that left a scar above your right eyebrow.

In addition to this imperfect symmetry, there must be something else at play. That something is chaos. While the order of symmetry may seem to be unrelated to chaos, this is not so. As Ian Stewart states in *What Shape Is a Snowflake?* (2001), "Symmetry and chaos are not mutually exclusive, but two sides of the same dynamical coin." This is when fractal geometry and chaos theory enter the scene (see "Orderly Chaos," page 270), taking us a few steps closer to seeing how order and chaos combine to delight us with the complex and astonishing essence of nature. In physics, it is the breaking of symmetry that explains the diversity of fundamental forces and particles. Without this complexity, the universe would be a very boring place. But without the order of symmetry, it would have no structure at all. Our cosmos are the dances of these partners.

HUMAN PATTERNS

We humans like patterns and sometimes see them even when they don't exist. We see animals in the canopy of stars and divine figures in burnt toast and coffee stains. As Ian Stewart points out, "Sometimes, though, it is our cherished patterns that prove to be the illusions." It's in our bones to be on the lookout for patterns, perhaps because pattern recognition brings pleasure along with self-preservation.

Opposite: While fingerprinting as a means of identification is giving way to more advanced methods such as DNA testing, fingerprints continue to be a symbolic illustration of uniqueness.

Find beauty not only in the thing itself but in the pattern of the shadows, the light and dark which that thing provides.

Jun'ichirō Tanizaki

For humans, the development of language has undoubtedly spawned much pleasure. Consider one of the first displays of body language developed by a child: smiling.

Who is immune to the infectious grin of an infant? We are naturally inclined to respond with a smile of our own, beginning the development of a wonderful pattern that offers unspoken cheer. As verbal language develops, the ability to express more intimate and complex thoughts is demonstrated, deepening the experience of life for both the initiator and recipient of exchanged ideas. Both verbal and nonverbal languages develop due to pattern recognition.

While recognizing patterns can enhance enjoyment of life, it also helps to ensure the continuation of a species. If we are out hiking, recognizing a pair of eyes with the familiar right–left symmetry comes in handy should we observe the stare of a cougar zeroing in on us. The same horizontal recognition might cue us in to a potential love interest casting an inviting glance from across the room. In his book *The Artful Universe* (1996), John D. Barrow writes, "The survival value of rapid pattern recognition is considerable."

Patterns we recognize come in many types, including (but not limited to) visual, auditory, conceptual, spatial, dynamical, and numerical. The more types we can incorporate into our repertoire, the better.

Maintaining a heads-up awareness led ancient peoples to recognize that when the sun reached a certain location in the sky, it was time to move south, where food was more plentiful and the climate more temperate. At some point, someone noticed that standing outside during a lightning storm increased chances of getting an unwanted charge out of life. Recognition of the black stripes on the bee comes in handy if we are allergic to bee stings.

Opposite: Close-up shot of a bee on a leaf.

> Where there is life there is pattern, and where there is pattern there is mathematics.

John D. Barrow

Paying heed to the repetitive nature of certain events can prevent us from repeating mistakes or help us to choose life-supporting behaviors. It is the attention given to observing patterns and habits that offers the possibility of liberation from suffering. Pain generated by certain behavior signals the need for cessation of a habit, while praise for excellent performance encourages continued efforts.

Any way you look at it, it pays to pay attention to patterns.

(Author's note: The study of patterns is a heady endeavor and can take an explorer in and out of the fields of science, philosophy, religion, and the social sciences. This book only lightly touches on some basic patterns. Should you find them of interest and wish to explore them more in depth, you will find many books on the subject, some of which are listed in the Bibliography.)

Patterns found in ice and fire formations illustrate the self-similar quality of fractals (see page 268).

Left: Ring of fire.

Opposite: Fernlike ice crystals form on the edge of a hole.

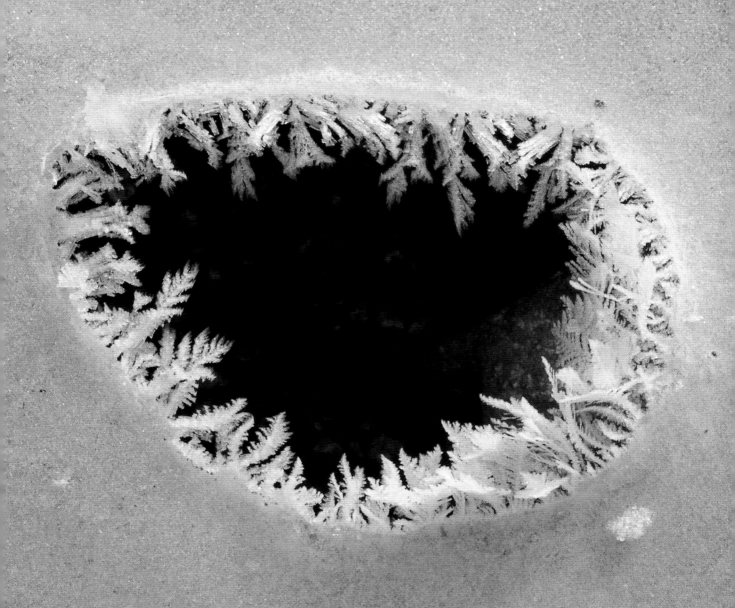

Branching

BRANCHING OUT

The pattern of branching expresses the mandala concept in an abstract fashion. Branches stemming from a tree's trunk, arterial pathways sprawling out from a city's central hub—both demonstrate outward expansion from an infinite center while simultaneously pointing back to the primal source from which they took form. The patterns created are not necessarily circular in shape; however, they do represent the nature of the mandala, a structure expanding from a limitless center.

From beginning to end, top to bottom, inside to out, branching supplies an efficient method for transporting energy to a large area. It provides a compromise between the spiral pattern, which provides the shortest overall line length to reach all destination points, and the starburst or radial pattern, which is the most direct method but uses more line length.

Flow is indicated when branching takes place. Phone trees are implemented when information needs to be spread quickly to a large number of people, and branching patterns are created by electrical discharges of lightning. Genetic heredity can be charted in the pattern of family trees in which branches can be drawn from parent to child to brothers, sisters, aunts, uncles, and cousins. And the branches of the United States government—executive, legislative, and judicial—were designed to ensure a balance of power.

Branching brings energy, growth, and expansion where needed. In nature, branching patterns are employed to send oxygen and blood to the cells of a body and to carry water from a flowing river to outlying areas.

Opposite: The atmospheric discharge of electricity creates a striking branching pattern.

For just as each new shoot on the tree grows out of the one preceding it, so the periods of history overlap, each stage germinating the one which is to come.

Roger Cook

Root systems of trees absorb nutrients from the soil and send them out to branches and leaves, which in turn collect energy from the sun. The continual feeding of small tributaries and streams into the larger flow of a river contributes to the creation of an entity greater than each part.

GROWING UP AND OUT

The mandalic nature of a tree's branching pattern is easy to see from a bird's-eye view. Stretching outward from the central trunk toward an imaginary circular boundary, branches gather sunlight while thirsty roots wind their way through soil in a similar pattern, seeking nourishment. Growth in each direction echoes the initial emergence of the plant from its seed. As new branches emerge at intervals in specific locations moving upward on the main stalk, each new branch faces a different direction than the one before. Each sprout is located in a different position both vertically and radially, creating a spiral pattern. The spacing of leaf growth in this way creates as little overlap of leaves as possible, ensuring that each leaf receives the maximum amount of sunshine.

SPIRALING CONNECTION

Branching is functionally connected to the Fibonacci sequence as well as to the regenerative pentagon, in which Φ makes its debut (see page 170). It is interesting to note that the degree of rotational spacing of leaves is 137.5, a number related to Φ.

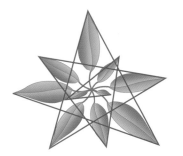

Left: A spiraling, mandalic pattern of growth is evident when a diagram is drawn over a leaf cluster. The order in which the leaves emerge create a branching pattern with spacing that relects the Fibonacci sequence.

Opposite: Macro shot of a leaf showing branching pattern.

This tree, wide as the heavens itself, has grown up into heaven from the earth. . . . It is the foundation of the round worlds, the center of the cosmos.

Hippolytus

Not only does the branching process reflect Φ, but also the flowers put out by the branches often contain numbers of petals found in the Fibonacci sequence (1, 1, 2, 3, 5, 8, 13. . .). The branching pattern is also closely associated with fractals. See page 174 for a discussion of the Fibonacci sequence.

BRANCHING AS SYMBOL

Every branch stems from a center, where it gives and receives energy and vitality. Symbolically, this center is seen as the *axis mundi*, or "axis of the world," an ancient concept that appears in various forms throughout many cultures and describes the central originating point of creation, as well as the separation and connection between the earth and the heavens. In artwork, it is often represented by a plant or tree and symbolizes the unification of the higher and lower realms comprised of the sky, earth, and underworld. A symbol of the axis mundi may also appear in buildings, such as Native American medicine lodges, that have central tent poles. Twentieth-century Romanian religious historian and philosopher Mircea Eliade says of the all-pervasive nature of a center: "Every Microcosm, every inhabited region, has a Center; that is to say, a place that is sacred above all." It is a center of being in which, as Hippolytus described in the third century CE, "all the diversities in our human nature are formed into a unity."

The tree of life is described by Mircea Eliade as the "symbolism of the Center." The axis mundi can also be seen as the body in which we grow—physically, mentally, and spiritually. The definition of a mandala also describes the body when viewed as "an integrated structure organized around a unifying center."

Opposite: *Union of Heaven and Earth*, by Jenny Speckels, 2008. The tree is often used as a symbol to represent the "axis mundi" or center from which creation takes place.

Looking inward is a straight line to the one, looking outward are multiple branches into the many. Yet, lest we forget, this whole tree is itself identical to the mysterious ineffable One transcending both one and many.

Thomas J. McFarlane

The heart is a central hub from which life-giving blood is circulated throughout our bodies by an intricate system of arteries and veins. Our spine symbolizes the central axis of our nervous system just as a symbolic heart is at the core of our emotional being. Old growth dies and falls away, making way for new growth. Obsolete ideas are replaced by new ones through the growth and expansion of our minds. The new branches that form from expanded awareness add strength to the tree and to our axis and base of being.

The branching pattern appears both above and below ground.

Top: Silhouette of trees; **bottom:** Roots of a young tree.

Opposite: Branching patterns are created when rivulets of water flow toward streams, eventually joining to create rivers.

At its base, the tree
is a single trunk,
representing the cosmic
axis, or axis mundi.
The branching of the
tree represents the
emanation of multiplicity
from unity. Despite this
branching, however,
the tree remains a
single, living organism.
Although apparently
divided, the tree is, and
always remains, whole.

Thomas J. McFarlane

LOOKING DEEPER

As we saw in Chapter 1, the appearance of the circle out of an infinite point is the necessary event from which form can manifest. The growth of a tree offers a metaphor for this mysterious occurrence, as well as for the evolving process of creation that follows. A tree (circle) takes its root in reality (the infinite point) and proceeds to manifest form (shapes). American mathematician Thomas J. McFarlane describes this transaction: "The worlds of form thus sprout and flower from the seed of distinction planted in the ground of Reality, freely branching out from the trunk in a self-similar manifestation of diverse possibility. This is the great tree of life."

Right from top: Electrical discharge was created by placing a block of Lucite in the six-megavolt electron beam of a linear accelerator. This type of fernlike, branching fractal structure is quite common in electricity; Microscopic shot of filamentous algae creating spores as a new filament rises from the central stem; Cholla cactus in Organ Pipe National Monument, Arizona.

Opposite: Sea fans in a colorful Mediterranean seabed.

CYCLES

CYCLE ANALYSIS

We inhale and exhale, our breath cycling in and out as an active mandala. Like a turning wheel, this cycle repeats itself, on average, between four and seven billion times during our life cycle. According to American scientist and mathematician Steven Strogatz, "At the heart of the universe is a steady, insistent beat, the sound of cycles in sync."

The word *cycle* is derived from the Greek word *kyklos*, meaning "circle," and is both a noun and a verb. Cycles come in a variety of types and sizes and convey a mandalic theme in either form or concept. On the grand scale, we observe that one cycle around the sun gives earthlings a year, while the moon's orbit indicates the passage of a month, and one complete turn on the earth's axis indicates that twenty-four hours have transpired. Indeed, all celestial objects within our galaxy are said to engage in continuous, circular movements that complete, and then repeat, themselves. At the microscale, atoms and molecules have cyclic vibrational modes that give them their unique signatures. The different colors of the rainbow are the cyclic vibrations of electromagnetic waves moving at faster or slower rates.

While they may help us mark time on our circular clocks, cycles are actually engaged in timelessness. The hands of a clock endlessly make their rounds, but the center of the clock remains constant—as in the mobile yet constant eye of a hurricane or the point around which a compass pivots. The constancy of center points reminds us of the infinite nature that lies at the center of the mandala, the place from which objects and activities spring, yet which itself remains unmoved.

Opposite: Time-lapse photography of the night sky reveals the circular pattern of star trails. This image shows the trails of southern stars over a nine-hour period in Namibia. The tree in the foreground is a quiver tree.

Full circle, from the tomb
of the womb to the
womb of the tomb, we
come: an ambiguous,
enigmatical incursion
into a world of solid
matter that is soon to
melt from us, like the
substance of a dream.

Joseph Campbell

It is this center point that embodies the quality of eternity, which infuses all movement with its timeless nature. As Plato said, "Time is the moving image of Eternity."

MOVING WITHIN CYCLES

The nature of cycles is to go round and round, creating dependable patterns that give us cues as to where or how to move. When our bike slows down, we pedal faster. We go when the traffic signal cycles to green. When the weather turns cold, blue whales head south for the tropics to breed, while some birds head north to escape winter in the southern hemisphere.

Our bodies also display cycles of movement. We circulate blood through our bodies using a cyclic pumping of the heart, and air flows in and out of our lungs in a respiratory cycle. A woman's menstrual cycle is a monthly event until she reaches menopause, which is yet another stage in her cycle of life. To get from here to there, a horse paces itself from an amble to a walk, from a trot to a gallop, and maybe into a full run, each gait executing a cycle of repeated leg movements with accompanying cycles of breath.

There is also the cycle of the Hero's Journey, a path we take daily and throughout our lives as we answer the call to adventures—be they as simple as moving through a day or making the commitment to follow a path to accomplish a personal goal. Indeed, our entire life cycle can be seen as a Hero's Journey.

Opposite: Sundials utilize a shadow-casting object called a gnomon to mark time according to the position of the sun. This garden sundial shows the time to be noon.

Even the seasons form a great circle in their changing, and always come back again to where they were. The life of a man is a circle from childhood to childhood, and so it is in everything where power moves.

Black Elk

The cyclical waxing and waning of our moon creates visual shapes that have long inspired artists to re-create these forms as symbols in their artwork, and calendar makers to create illustrative icons for almanacs and calendars. Similarly, cyclical seasonal changes influence the colors with which we clothe our bodies and the foods we put on our tables.

Cycles are at the root of the circular nature of life and keep us in touch with its impermanence. They both spring from and recoil into an ineffable origin—and then they cycle all over again.

Top: Four of the stages of a dandelion's life cycle.

Above left: Image showing the metamorphosis of a butterfly from pupa to adult. The life cycle of butterflies consists of four stages: egg, caterpillar (larva), pupa (chrysalis), adult (imago).

Above right: In temperate locations, a year follows the seasonal cycle of spring, summer, fall, and winter.

Opposite: The cycles of the moon, or lunar phases, occur as the moon orbits the earth and the earth orbits the sun. Changing positions of the earth, moon, and sun cause the observer to see varying amounts of the moon.

Waves

WAVING BACK

Like drops of water in the ocean, each of us participates in the creation of waves that weave the fabric of the universe. Our vocal chords vibrate, making sound waves that emerge through our mouths and noses as audible expressions. Even when our bodies appear still, the atoms of which they are composed are quivering, creating waves. When we move, we cause air to be displaced, resulting in a rippling effect. Some waves we can see and hear, most we cannot, yet they all assume the timeless shape of the circle—manifesting in time and space, co-creating the mandala of life.

A physical wave is a pattern of energy moving through a medium such as air or liquid. Although this energy may travel a long distance through the medium, the medium itself only experiences localized oscillations. An example of this phenomenon can occasionally be seen in a sports stadium. Energized fans participate in creating a wave pattern by jumping up in groups, then sitting back down in a sequence that travels around the stadium. The wave moves through the crowd, but no one leaves their seat except to stand up. Similarly, the sound waves of their cheers are small localized back and forth movements of individual air molecules. The energy of the sound travels across the stadium through compression waves, even when the air is still.

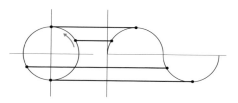

Left: The shape of a wave is a repeated mathematical pattern showing consistent intervals of time and distance. To see how the circle plays a part in the creation of a wave, imagine drawing a circle on a piece of paper while the paper is pulled slowly from underneath your pencil. A wave is created.

Opposite: Photographers use diffraction filters that are etched with tiny lines to create rainbow halo effects.

. . . and there, in the midst of the light, they saw the ends of the chains of heaven let down from above: for this light is the belt of heaven, and holds together the circle of the universe.

Plato

Vibrations of particles and fields in various frequencies and wavelengths comprise the world we experience through our senses. Everything is vibrating, creating waves of energy that are spreading out into the universe in the forms of light, heat, and sound. The wave family of the electromagnetic spectrum creates a complex weave of intermingling patterns.

In addition to visible light waves, the wave family of the electromagnetic spectrum includes radio waves, microwaves, infrared waves, ultraviolet waves, X-rays, and gamma waves. A circular expression of wave pattern is seen in the generation of electricity, which involves the rotation of a conductor within a magnetic field. As Robert Lawlor states in his book *Sacred Geometry: Philosophy and Practice* (1989), "the entire perceptible universe is composed of vibrations, perceived by us as wave phenomena."

Wave theory is linked to quantum physics and provides a fascinating topic worthy of deeper study. It is included here because of its importance in the overall structure of the universe—the mandala in which we live—and is therefore integral to the topic of mandalas. Here we will simply touch upon a few visual manifestations.

Opposite: Circular halos are an optical phenomenon produced when light is reflected and refracted by ice crystals.

Making the Invisible Visible

Just as wind creates ripples on a pond, the pulsations of sound propagating through air or water also create patterns. In the 1960s, Swiss doctor Hans Jenny researched how audible sound shapes inert substances into structured, yet always fluid, forms. He named this field Kymatik (Cymatics, in English), from the Greek word for "wave," *Kyma*.

Precise patterns can be created in water as it is vibrated at specific audible frequencies. Even though the water is in a constant state of agitation due to the sound pulsations, coherent standing wave forms will remain intact as long as the frequency (pitch) and amplitude (volume) of the animating tone is maintained . . . just as we maintain a sense of ourselves despite all of the influences (vibrations) constantly assailing us.

Visualize yourself as a mandala of the five elements: water, earth, air, fire, and ether. Can you see your own life as a coherent whole, comprised of many disparate elements, all mysteriously held together by an ineffable bond?

The complex symmetrical and geometric forms seen in cymatic images bear a striking resemblance to patterns found in nature, yet they are actually light interacting with standing waves in water. These standing waves, a result of resonance, develop in response to audible sound "animating" water in a small, shallow retaining plate.

Above from top: Cymatics image; Tulip; Cymatics image; *Mammillaria microthele* cactus.

Opposite: Cymatics image.

All forms of radiation—light, sound, heat, or electromagnetism—propagate by means of oscillation or pulsation, which frequently appear as waves. Depending on the medium they move through, and their frequency, we may perceive them as light, sound, or not at all, at least through our conventional five senses.

Within the gross vibration of flesh is the fine vibration of the cosmic current, the life energy, and permeating both flesh and life energy is the most subtle vibration, that of consciousness.

Paramahansa Yogananda

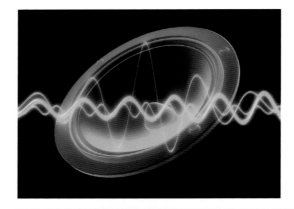

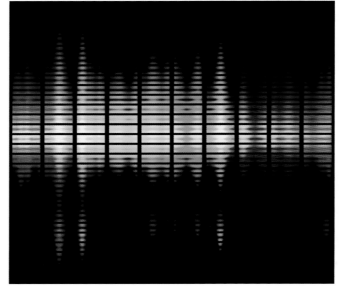

Above: Sound is a traveling wave composed of frequencies that are within hearing range.

Left: The colors of the rainbow are visible light waves—the only electromagnetic waves we can see.

Opposite: Each ripple extends outward from the source to infinity. As ripples interact, they create entirely new and unique wave textures, forms, and structures. This occurs at every scale of magnitude, from interpenetrating universes to valence rings within a hydrogen atom.

266

Fractals

ON AND ON AND . . .

While a fractal image may not immediately bring to mind the visual representation of a mandala, the topic is included here because fractals are integral to the story of shapes and patterns. Fractals and circles offer a glimpse into the boundless world of self-similarity. Just as a mandala exemplifies the never-ending possibility of expansion and contraction from and into the infinite, so too does a fractal. Each displays limitless self-similarity when magnified; concentric circles zero in toward an infinite center just as the pattern of a fractal design reveals ever smaller and smaller versions of itself upon closer inspection.

Fractals don't explain the phenomenon of creation, but they do describe an aspect of the exquisite growth process that leads to creation. We don't know why the point suddenly emerged from the infinite or why the perfect solution to a problem pops into our heads after weeks of consternation, but we can talk about how the process appears to evolve. There is a reason scientists strive to be on the cutting edge of their professions and why artists like to push boundaries: that is where beauty and truth are revealed, and where fractals grow.

Fractal is a term coined by Benoît Mandelbrot, a French-American mathematician considered to be the founder of fractal geometry. It is a rough or uneven geometric shape that when subdivided is, at least approximately, a smaller-size copy of the whole.

Opposite: Queen Anne's lace is a delicate example of a floral fractal. Each of the tiny blossoms extending out from the center resembles the larger flower.

Clouds are not spheres, mountains are not cones, coastlines are not circles, and bark is not smooth, nor does lightning travel in a straight line.

Benoît Mandelbrot

Fractals are patterns that can be generated using mathematical equations and also manifest in nature. The amazing feature of fractal images is that no matter how fractured the pattern appears to be, repeated magnification reveals the same self-similar pattern. In nature, we can observe this feature on the surface of a rock that, upon closer inspection, resembles the hillside from which it came. Further magnification reveals even tinier patterns on the rock that mimic the craggy hillside. This characteristic can also be seen in the nature of the point and its ability to offer a glimpse into the ever-unfolding story of infinity. When viewing a fractal or a point, we can zoom in or out to find an infinite expression of . . . well, the infinite.

ORDERLY CHAOS

Fractal science is used to model phenomena for study in the fields of science and statistics in order to understand complex and seemingly disordered systems in nature. For example, the branching of the circulatory system that carries blood throughout our body, when magnified, reveals a self-similar pattern.

The study of the dynamics of sensitive systems that appear unpredictable or disordered is called chaos theory. It is the attempt to find pattern, or an underlying order, in what appears to be patternless, such as weather. In his book *Fractals: The Pattern of Chaos* (1992), John Briggs states that the "study of chaos is also the study of wholeness." He goes on to say that the study of chaos theory and fractal geometry has "opened up undreamed of correspondences between the abstract mental realm of mathematics and the movements and shapes of our planet's myriad organisms."

Examples of the fractal pattern of self-similarity abound in nature. When viewed zoomed in or zoomed out, each image pictured here reveals a similar pattern.

Opposite—**top row:** Fern frond, tree branches against the sky, aerial view of a cliff along the coast of Maui, Hawaii; **center row:** Blue sky with clouds, macro shot of Romanesco broccoli, a variant form of cauliflower; **bottom row:** Aerial view of the Namib Desert, spanning Namibia and southwest Angola, aerial view of fjords in Alaska.

In the case of fractal patterns, we are exposed to a highly developed form of organized pattern that is also present in the natural world (in leaves, trees, and rock formations); it is therefore not surprising that our ability to identify, sort, and classify patterns is activated and engrossed by fractal works of art.

John D. Barrow

From Chapter 1: "Circles: Concentric," you'll recall that Edward Lorenz coined the phrase *butterfly effect* as a term to describe the major impact that even the tiniest event can have on a large system. Like a grain of sand in an oyster that agitates and instigates the production of a pearl, even a tiny event can push order into chaos and catapult a system into the act of creation.

An example from everyday life might look like this: Things are going along nicely when you are confronted with a situation that requires attention. It's a perturbing problem and you might even avoid dealing with it for a while—until it gets bigger. And then bigger. Finally you are forced to come up with a solution. You struggle with the process until suddenly it becomes apparent what must be done. You implement your solution and things settle down into a more orderly state, though you now have grown in experience, which enriches you and those around you. The dilemma with which you were confronted forced you to create a solution, and in that process you were forced to grow—to let go of wanting things as they were in favor of accepting things as they are and, from there, accepting your ability to change and create something new.

Upon closer inspection, the mountain and rock each reveal edges with similar craggy patterns.

Right: The earth's entire outer solid layer, the lithosphere, is composed of rock.

Opposite: The Matterhorn, located in the Pennine Alps between Switzerland and Italy, is one of the largest mountains in the Alps.

I believe the geometric proportion served the Creator as an idea when He introduced the continuous generation of similar objects from similar objects.

Homer Smith

We can see the process of creation as a cycle involving four stages: 1. Order (everything is fine); 2. Disruption of order by an internal or external force (a situation develops that creates tension and requires action); 3. Instability and chaos (response is forced, creation takes place); and 4. Reorganization (the system adapts to the new situation in which equilibrium and balance are restored . . . at least until the next growth spurt occurs).

All elements appear to be engaged in constant interaction with each other, affecting and contributing to an ongoing flow of events, which at times appears chaotic but which results in an enigmatic type of order.

THE WILD FRONTIER

It's all about boundaries. That's where the edge-pushers are actively engaged in exploring uncharted territories in science and art. Tension between the whole and the part is needed in order for creation to take place, and that's what boundaries offer: the tension necessary for growth and creation.

At the boundary, tension on the outside is intimately connected with the tension being created on the inside, generating a self-similar pattern and shape. If you push inwards on a balloon, a reciprocal shape is formed on the inside that matches the outside—the interior reflects the exterior. That's where those intricate, self-similar patterns are generated in the fractal models.

Mathematician Thomas J. McFarlane describes the stage of transition from order to chaos as the fractal boundary, "the region of magical beauty, the region of creation. At this boundary, we lose the distinction between part and whole."

Opposite: The repetitive growth pattern of this succulent gives it fractal-like qualities.

274

As above,
so below.

The Emerald Tablet of
Hermes

This is where the magic of creation takes place—in a place of wonder that cannot be quantified or qualified, just as we find in the center of the mandala. It is an extraordinary and enthralling chaos that is born out of, and with, order. It is the moment in which we are enlivened by a thought or act that appears to emerge not from our own mind but from some unnamable place, such as when the perfect word emerges in a poem or an impeccable brush stroke hits the canvas. It is a place that seems wild and exploding with potential and potency. It is a climax of creation and it's a good thing: it's how we grow.

After a new creation emerges, a breath is taken and there is a return to order. But it is a new order, one that reflects fresh growth and, if treated with care, can continue to reveal more beauty.

FRACTAL IMAGES

The creative process offers another perspective on the reflective nature of fractals. Author John Briggs refers to the artist's ability to employ fractal concepts to express their personal and unique vision of wholeness as *reflectaphors*. Similar to metaphors, reflectaphors contain both similarities and differences. He describes the reflectaphor as "a juxtaposition of terms that are both self-similar and different and as a result help open the mind."

Right: Computer-generated fractal swirl.

Opposite: The Fibonacci spiral of this begonia leaf
illustrates the repetitive pattern of a fractal similar
to the computer-generated illustration.

You have to
be inordinately
insensitive to how
scientific progress
works to dismiss the
fractal geometry
of nature as some
kind of unimportant
coincidence.

Ian Stuart

In a musical composition, the fractal tension created by a reflectaphor might be heard in a series of notes played by one instrument, then echoed by another in an unusual way. In visual art, reflectaphors create a captivating tension when two different elements, similar in form or color (such as a winding road and a wandering stream) are placed in just the right proximity to each other so as to create a reflective, yet surprising effect—reminiscent of the captivating, intricate boundaries seen in fractals. Thomas J. McFarlane refers to this edge as the place where "dialectical tension is manifested in its mathematical form, and it is our love for its beauty that drives us toward it, toward creation."

REFLECTIONS

"The Mandelbrot fractal portrays in two dimensions the infinity between zero and one, the potential and the actual . . . [His] formula provides a mathematical map to navigate in the crack between the worlds, to cope with Chaos and bring our potential into actuality," writes Arnold Keyserling, a twentieth-century German philosopher and author.

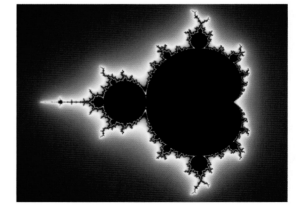

Right: The intricate edges of the Mandelbrot fractal can be infinitely magnified to reveal an iterative pattern.

Opposite: The decorative round, bumpy shapes on this sea urchin skeleton create fractal patterns.

Because of its ability to intimate worlds within worlds, art has always been fractal.

John Briggs

While far too complex a subject to be covered in any depth here, I have presented fractals to tantalize you toward further exploration and offer a taste of what they bring to the complex nature of life as it unfolds from the unbounded center of the mandala.

Fractals and chaos theory offer a window into a world that is diverse and wild, yet connected and unified—the world in which we live. Computer formulas can describe some of its complexity, but it is the untamed nature of life that makes the world come alive. John Briggs suggests we should exercise caution in how we see and use fractals, not to conjecture that the world can be controlled, or even understood. To the contrary, he advises, "Fractals and chaos tell us about the inherent value of living in a world that springs beyond our control." While we observe an appearance of order in nature, it is also important to remember that the infinite nature of a fractal is itself a reflection of the point to which we cannot point, the no-thing from which all things spring. Nature is not necessarily something to be controlled or mechanized; it is something to behold.

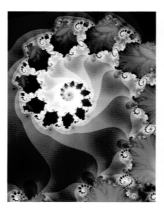 

Above: This computer-generated fractal captures a similar energy seen in the two artworks pictured here.

The chaotic turbulence of nature is expressed as an iterative pattern in both Vincent van Gogh's painting *Starry Night* (1889), **above,** and Japanese artist Hokusai's woodblock print *Great Wave off Kanagawa* (ca. 1830–32), **opposite**. Known for the fractal nature of his artwork, Hokusai used similar patterns at various scales in this work.

AFTERWORD

The universe isn't flying apart. It's flying together.

JED McKENNA

We began the journey with a point and, having traversed its myriad expressions, we have come full circle to *this* point. Where does that leave us? Right where we started—in the center of our own mandala, where in every moment we experience the complex, magnificent, interconnected nature of life and where it is possible to pursue an even deeper experience of who and what we are in the universe.

We have seen the infinite point take form in nature as shapes from micro to macro, embellished by patterns that can be described by mathematics and physics. All things are connected by a shared structural component: an atom, at the center of which we find no-thing. Some atoms appear as material objects in our visual field, others as invisible gases, but all are things whose center appears empty. From the atoms that make up our bodies to the air that surrounds us, we see that there is no end to me and no beginning to you—we are all connected at a fundamental level. And we are made of things whose centers are no-thing. The interrelated quality of all things creates "an integrated structure that is organized around a unifying center" of an infinite point—a mandala.

From the most fundamental to the most grand, all things are composed of mandalas. Each shares a quality of emptiness and contributes to the creation of one vast, infinite mandala of which our finite minds cannot conceive. After all, it's hard to conceive of nothing. And yet, we do observe phenomena.

While we can discuss the phenomena that appear to arise in the objective world, it is important to keep in mind that what we are describing is an aspect of the whole as well as the whole itself. Unity (the circle) is like a tree trunk, with each branch stemming from it representing a part, as well as the whole, of the tree. We ourselves are both the diversity within unity and unity itself, and are viewing a world that springs from a place to which no one can point—everything we see is a reflection of the infinite point.

Just as when we seek to penetrate matter, the further we go, the more we find only boundless space. So also, when we seek to penetrate the depths of our being, we find no boundaries. At the center of our personal mandala lies a spaceless, dimensionless, pure awareness. The phenomena we observe are manifestations of no-thing. Our consciousness is the only *thing* we can experience that we can absolutely know..

Mystics of all world religions have stated that meditation on the infinite point—the idea of no-thing—can ultimately lead to an awareness of the highest state of being, Enlightenment. American author and spiritual teacher Joel Morwood describes this awareness as the realization that the "appearance of an objective world distinguishable from a subjective self is but the imaginary form in which Consciousness Perfectly Realizes Itself." The objects and boundaries we think we see are illusions. According to the theory of the Cartesian Theater, established by American philosopher Daniel Dennett, these illusions provide us with a theater in which we can view the drama of life. In addition, our personal theaters can offer us the opportunity to see that the drama is in truth a projection on an imaginary screen, similar to being in a dream. Mystics tell us that, with commitment and determination to see the truth of reality, it is possible to leave the theater of dreams and awaken to the realization that we are surrounded by the infinite and we *are* the infinite. Everything is connected; everything changes. Pay attention.

Mandalas for Drawing

This book has explored the mandala as it appears in our visual field and has described it as a tool for personal growth and expression. One way to use a mandala as a tool for introspection or relaxation is to make one. We can explore the terrain of our deepest thoughts and emotions to find meaningful symbols that reveal our current state of mind, then carefully translate them into a fine artwork. Or we can simply enjoy doodling with colored pens or pencils in a kaleidoscopic mandala pattern. Either way, mandala-making is a process that offers the opportunity to reflect, create, and relax.

Mandalas can be made using a variety of methods and mediums. We have included these predrawn mandalas for coloring because they serve as an easy and simple entry into the world of mandala-making. As a meditative activity, you can color them carefully while focusing your energy and attention inward. Or use them to make a quick, colorful splash of expression that satisfies the urge to create art without the need for purchasing special art supplies. Just the simple act of coloring a mandala can be a fun, relaxing experience. For best results, make a photocopy of each mandala you would like to color and do your coloring on the photocopy. Enjoy!

Acknowledgments

Many thanks to the following people. . .

Barbara Berger, my editor at Sterling, for the opportunity to further explore the mandala and work (again) with a wonderful editor who, with the soul of an artist, visualizes possibilities and shapes words into readable art. Thank you, Barbara! Sasha Tropp, who, with Sherlockian skill, identified unidentified objects, honed text, and added many tasteful touches. Both were infinitely patient with an author compelled to change and rearrange. Also at Sterling, I owe thanks to Mary Hern, production editor, Jason Chow, cover designer, and Gavin Motnyk, interior designer.

I am grateful to the following people:

Michael S. Schneider (www.constructingtheuniverse.com), whose wonderful book, *A Beginner's Guide to Constructing the Universe*, (which I highly recommend), has been an important inspiration personally, as well as in the creation of this book. I credit Michael for curing my math phobia and opening my eyes to the wondrous world of sacred geometry.

Chara Curtis, my textual midwife, supreme hand-holder, and dear friend who helped birth this book in many ways. I cannot thank her enough (but I can try!). Tom McFarlane, whose science, math, and spiritual expertise added accuracy, clarity, and oh-so-much depth to the text. He provided on-call, invaluable input seasoned with sumptuous insights, for which I am truly grateful.

Professor Larry S. Liebovitch, who kindly vetted the information in Chapter "Circle: Eyes." Jeff Volk (www.cymaticsource.com), for his "wavy" expertise, consultation, and verbiage contribution to the wave section.

Mom and Dad, who nurtured my artistic spirit. Devo, for sharp, tasty commentary, served up fat-free with gusto. Rien, for squaring C4, critter IDs, and living the inspiring metaphor of a rising phoenix. Gavon, who sees the universe at work in creepy, crawly things and reminds me to wonder.

Sheila Craven, whose keen eyes improved the text and good nature kept me smiling. Arlene Carlson House, Meredith McIlmoyle, and Jackie Heinricher for friendship and cheerleading.

Pamela Turczyn, whose beautiful artworks add grace and depth to the book, and Maggie Macnab, for sharing her Chapter 0 title and cool horse logo. Vandorn Hinnant and A. T. Mann for eleventh-hour art contributions.

Joel Morwood, my teacher, who points the way.

And, my husband, David, who provided me with the amazing gift to write in peace and comfort while he brought home the bacon. His amazing insights enhanced the text and, with loving support, he helped make the creation of this book possible. I married well.

Bibliography/Resources

Argüelles, José and Miriam. *Mandala*, Boston: Shambhala, 1995.

Aurobindo, Sri. *The Life Divine*. Twin Lakes, WI: Lotus Press, 2000.

Barrow, John D. *The Artful Universe: The Cosmic Source of Human Creativity*. New York: Little, Brown and Company, 1995.

———. *Impossibility: The Limits of Science and the Science of Limits*. New York: Oxford University Press, 1999.

Belloli, Jay, ed. *The Universe: A Convergence of Art, Music and Science*. London: Reaktion Books, 2001.

Brauen, Martin. *The Mandala: Sacred Circle in Tibetan Buddhism*. Boston: Shambhala, 1998.

Briggs, John. *Fractals: The Patterns of Chaos*. New York: Simon & Schuster, 1992.

Campbell, Joseph. *The Hero's Journey*. Novato, CA: New World Library, 2003.

Capra, Fritjof. *The Web of Life*. New York: Doubleday, 1996.

Carpenter, Kenneth. *Eggs, Nests and Baby Dinosaurs*. Bloomington: Indiana University Press, 1999.

Chögyam, Ngakpa and Déchen, Khandro. *Spectrum of Ecstasy*. Ramsey, NJ: Aro Books, 1997.

Cook, John and Andrus, Ethel Percy. *The Book of Positive Quotations*. Minneapolis: Fairview Press, 2007.

Cook, Roger. *The Tree of Life*. New York: Thames & Hudson, 1974.

Cooper, J.C. *An Illustrated Encyclopaedia of Traditional Symbols*. New York: Thames & Hudson, 1978.

Cornell, Judith. *Mandala: Luminous Symbols for Healing*. Wheaton, IL: Theosophical Publishing House, 1994.

Cunningham, Bailey. *Mandala: Journey to the Center*. New York: DK Publishing, 2002.

Devlin, Keith J. *Mathematics: The Science of Patterns*. New York: Macmillan, 1996.

Doczi, György. *The Power of Limits*. Boston: Shambhala, 1994.

Eliade, Mircea, Apostolos-Cappadona, Diane, eds. *Symbolism, the Sacred, and the Arts*. New York: Continuum International Publishing Group, 1992.

Encyclopedia of Eastern Philosophy and Religion. Boston: Shambhala, 1984.

Fincher, Susanne F. *Creating Mandalas*. Boston: Shambhala, 1991.

Fox, Matthew. *Illuminations of Hildegard of Bingen*. Rochester: Bear & Company,Inc., 1985.

Gielis, Johan. *Inventing the Circle: The Geometry of Nature*. Antwerp: Geniaal bvba, 2003.

Huang, Tao. *Laoism: The Complete Teachings of Lao Zi*. Atlanta: Humanics Ltd., 2001.

Huyser, Anneke, *Mandala Workbook*. Haarlem, The Netherlands: Binkey Kok Publications, 2002.

Huxley, Francis. *The Eye: The Seer and the Seen*. New York: Thames & Hudson, 1990.

Iamblichus and Waterfield, Robin. *The Theology of Arithmetic*. Newburyport, MA: Red Wheel / Weiser, 1988.

Icon Group International (compiler). *Manifestoes: Webster's Quotations, Facts and Phrases*. San Diego: Icon Group International, 2008.

Juster, Norton. *The Dot and the Line*. Nashville: Thomas Nelson Printers Ltd., 1963.

Jung, C. G. *Archetypes and the Collective Unconscious*, New Jersey: Princeton University Press, 1981.

———. *Collected Works: Psychology and Religion: West and East, Volume 11*. New Jersey: Princeton University Press, 1975.

———. *Man and His Symbols*. London: Aldus Books Ltd., 1964.

———. *Mandala Symbolism*. New Jersey: Princeton University Press, 1973.

———. *Word and Image*. New Jersey: Princeton University Press, 1979.

Kaplan, Robert and Ellen Kaplan. *The Nothing That Is: A Natural History of Zero*. New York: Oxford University Press, 1999.

Kardos, Edward G. *Zen Master Next Door*. Lake Worth, FL: Humanics Publishing Group, 2009.

Khanna, Madhu. *Yantra: The Tantric Symbol of Cosmic Unity*. New York: Thames & Hudson, Ltd., 1979.

Lao Tzu, Gia-Fu Feng, Jane English. *Tao Te Ching*. New York: Vintage Books, 1972.

Lawlor, Robert. *Sacred Geometry*. New York: Thames & Hudson, Ltd., 1982.

Lauterwasser, Alexander. *Water Sound Images: The Creative Music of the Universe*. Newmarket, NH: MACROmedia, 2007.

Leidy, Denise Patry and Robert A. F. Thurman. *Mandala: The Architecture of Enlightenment*. New York: Thames & Hudson, Ltd., 1997.

Liebovitch, Larry. "Why the Eye is Round," in *Advances in Organ Biology*, vol. 10: *The Biology of the Eye*, Ed. J. Fischbarg, pp. 1–19. New York: Elsevier, 2006.

Liungman, Carl G. *Dictionary of Symbols*. New York: W. W. Norton & Company, 1991.

Livio, Mario. *The Golden Ratio: The Story of Phi: The World's Most Astonishing Number*. New York: Random House, Inc., 2003.

Longchenpa. *You Are the Eyes of the World*. Translated by Merrill Peterson and Kennard Lipman. Ithaca, NY: Snow Lion Publications, 2000.

Lundquist, John M. *Meeting Place of Heaven and Earth*. New York: Thames & Hudson, 1993.

Mann, A. T. *Sacred Architecture*. Rockport, ME: Element Books, Ltd., 1993.

McFarlane, Thomas J. *Sacred Science: Essays on Mathematics, Physics and Spiritual Philosophy*. www.integralscience.org/sacredscience/SS_title.html.

———. *Einstein and Buddha: The Parallel Sayings*. Berkeley, CA: Ulysses Press, 2002.

MacNab, Maggie. *Decoding Design*. Cincinnati: HOW Books, 2008.

Morwood, Joel. *Naked Through the Gate*. Eugene, OR: Center for Sacred Sciences, 1985.

———. *The Way of Selflessness: A Practical Guide to Enlightenment Based on the Teachings of the World's Great Mystics*. Eugene, OR: Center for Sacred Sciences, 2009.

Murphy, Pat. *By Nature's Design*. San Francisco: Chronicle Books, 1993.

Plato. *Timaeus*. Translated by Benjamin Jowett. Middlesex, UK: The Echo Library, 2006.

Plato. *The Republic*. Translated by Desmond Lee. New York: Penguin Books, 2003.

Proclus. *Proclus: A Commentary on the First Book of Euclid's Elements*. Translated by Glenn. R Morrow. New Jersey: Princeton University Press, 1992.

Purce, Jill. *The Mystic Spiral: Journey of the Soul*. New York: Thames & Hudson, 1974.

Schneider, Michael S. *A Beginner's Guide to Constructing the Universe*. New York: HarperCollins, 1994.

Seife, Charles and Matt Zimet. *Zero: The Biography of a Dangerous Idea*. New York: Penguin, 2000.

Skinner, Stephen. *Sacred Geometry: Deciphering the Code*. New York: Sterling Publishing, 2009

Stewart, Ian. *What Shape is a Snowflake?* East Sussex, UK: The Ivy Press, Ltd., 2001.

Strogatz, Steven H. *SYNC: The Emerging Science of Spontaneous Order*. New York: Hyperion, 2003.

Teresi, Dick, *Lost Discoveries: The Ancient Roots of Modern Science, from the Babylonians to the Maya*. New York: Simon & Schuster, 2003.

Trungpa, Chögyam. *Dharma Art*. Boston: Shambhala Publications, 1996.

———. *Orderly Chaos: The Mandala Principle*. Boston: Shambhala Publications, 1981.

Wilhelm, Richard. *The Secret of the Golden Flower*. New York: Harvest Books, 1962.

ARTIST WEB SITES

Lori Bailey Cunningham: www.mandalaproject.org

Daniel Dancer: www.inconcertwithnature.com

Maggie Macnab: www.macnabdesign.com

A.T. Mann: www.atmann.net

P.C. Turczyn: www.pcturczyn.com

Vandorn Hinnan: www.lightweavings.com

Index

PICTURE CREDITS

COURTESY WIKIMEDIA COMMONS:

Frontispiece: Helix Nebula, 2003/Author: NASA, NOAO, ESA, the Hubble Helix Nebula Team, M. Meixner (STScI), and T.A. Rector (NRAO); 6 (tl): Painted nineteenth-century Tibetan mandala of the Naropa tradition, Vajrayogini stands in the center of two crossed red triangles, Rubin Museum of Art, New York; 11: The Whirlpool Galaxy (Spiral Galaxy M51, NGC 5194), 2005/Author: NASA and European Space Agency; 52 (t): Cultures of various strains of a destructive plant mold called Phomopsis/Author: Scott Bauer; 82 (tl): Cluster of green wine grapes; Author: Martin Kozák; 86 (br): Orb-weaver spider (*Argiope*) pictured on Ulugur Mountains in Tanzania/Author: Muhammad Mahdi Karim (www.micro2macro.net); 114 (b): Cover of the Chalice Well, depicting the Vescia Piscis, in Glastonbury, Somerset, England/Author: Theangryblackwoman at http://en.wikipedia.org; 136 (b): Runestone, featuring a triquetra, standing in the University Park of Uppsala in Sweden; 138 (bc): Looking out of a north-facing window of the Chrysler Building, New York/Author: Julius Schorzman; 141 (tr): *The Legs of Man* by Bryan Kneale, in front of the passenger terminal at Ronaldsway Airport on the Isle of Man, British Isles/Author: Gregory J Kingsley; 154 (first): Computer-illustrated tetrahedron/Author: User:DTR; 154 (second): Computer-illustrated hexahedron/Author: User:DTR; 154 (third): Computer-illustrated octahe-dron/Author: User:Stannered; 154 (fourth): Computer-illustrated icosahedron/Author: User:DTR; 154 (fifth): Computer-illustrated dodecahedron/Author: User:DTR; 158 (l): Rubik's cube/Author: Booyabazooka; 181: Restored image of Leonardo da Vinci's *Mona Lisa*, 1503–1505, Musée du Louvre, Paris; 189 (tl): Drudenfuss, a "magical" symbol on a house in Ahrweiler, Germany, dating from 1639/Author: Ramessos; 191 (cr): Scarlet milkweed flowers/Author: Dohduhdah; 195: View from space of a low pressure system off the southwestern coast of Iceland, 2003/Author: NASA; 202 (bl): Feather star (*Lamprometra sp.*)/Author: Nhobgood; 204 (tr): Romanesque door of the parish church in Pürgg, Styria, Austria, decorated with spirals believed to defend the church against evil spirits/Author: Marion Schneider & Christoph Aistleitner; 204 (b): Design for the *Tree of Life* by Gustav Klimt, featured on a frieze in the dining room of the Stoclet Palace in Brussels, Belgium; 206 (ml): Tendril of a purple passionflower (*Passiflora incarnata*)/Author: Avicentegil; 210 (t): Most common form of the "Flower of Life" hexagonal pattern, made up of 19 complete circles and 36 partial circular arcs, enclosed by a large circle; 216 (l): Roman mosaic from the city of El Djem in Tunisia, a former Roman settle-ment/Author: GIRAUD Patrick; 218 (r): Honeycomb grouper (*Epinephelus merra*)/Author: jon hanson (http://flickr.com/people/61952179@N00) from London, UK; 220 (br): Six-sided feature encircling the north pole of Saturn, taken by the Cassini orbiter in 2006/Credit: NASA/JPL/University of Arizona; 275: *Crassula capiatella*, a variety of succulent/Author: Eric Hunt; 280 (r): *The Starry Night* by Vincent van Gogh, 1889, Museum of Modern Art, New York; 281: *Kanagawa oki nami ura* ("The Great Wave Off Shore of Kanagawa") by Katsushika Hokusai, 1832.

SHUTTERSTOCK:

© Shutterstock/Tom Gundy: vi; © Shutterstock/lynnlin: xvi; © Shutterstock/Joshua Haviv: 1; © Shutterstock/Christopher Marin: 2 (l); © Shutterstock/paul prescott: 2 (r); © Shutterstock/Julie Hucke: 3 © Shutterstock/basel101658: 4; © Shutterstock/zimowa: 5; © Shutterstock/Ngo Thye Aun: 6 (tr); © Shutterstock/Ron Zmiri: 6 (l); © Shutterstock/Artur Bogacki: 8 (t & c); © Shutterstock/Regien Paassen: 8 (b); © Shutterstock/BESTWEB: 9; © Shutterstock/mehmetcan: 14 (b); © Shutterstock/Judy Crawford: 15 (tl); © Shutterstock/VOJTa Herout: 15 (tr); © Shutterstock/Antoine Beyeler: 15 (br); © Shutterstock/Luciano Mortula: 16 (t); © Shutterstock/Desmond D: 16 (bc); © Shutterstock/John Lock: 16 (br); © Shutterstock/Varina and Jay Patel: 17; © Shutterstock/Khoo Si Lin: 18 (r); © Shutterstock/Olga Lyubkina: 20; © Shutterstock/WizData, inc.: 21; © Shutterstock/Ciurzynski: 22 (tl); © Shutterstock/Gordan Milic: 22 (b); © Shutterstock/John A. Anderson: 22 (tr); © Shutterstock/Tim Mainiero: 23 © Shutterstock/Oliver Lenz Fotodesign: 25 (tl); ©

PICTURE CREDITS

THE ART ARCHIVE

PHOTO RESEARCHERS

Researchers, Inc.; 221: M.I. Walker/Photo Researchers, Inc.; 252 (t): Ted Kinsman/Photo Researchers, Inc.

WAVES-CYMATICS:

264 (t): Hans Jenny, from *Cymatics: A Study of Wave Phenomena and Vibration*, © 2001 MACROmedia Publishing, NH USA. www.cymaticsource.com
264 (bc): Hans Jenny, from *Cymatics: A Study of Wave Phenomena and Vibration*, © 2001 MACROmedia Publishing, NH USA. www.cymaticsource.com
265: © 2002 Alexander Lauterwasser, From *Water Sound Images*, MACROmedia Publishing, Newmarket, NH USA. www.cymaticsource.com

GETTY IMAGES:

[Ezra Shaw/Staff]/Getty Images: 14 (t); [Luca Zampedri/NonStock]/Getty Images: 36 (r); [nanolytics Austria]/Getty Images: 50 (r); [Spike Walker]/Getty Images: 63; [Mark Schneider]/Getty Images: 155; [Kim Steele]/Getty Images: 205; [G. Wanner]/Getty Images: 211; [Harry Taylor]/Getty Images: 222 (t)

ARTISTS:

Daniel Dancer: 15 (bl); Maggie Macnab :16 (bl); P. C. Turczyn: 19, 31, 47, 67, 161; 175: Vandorn Hinnant, 2009

AUTHOR (BAILEY CUNNINGHAM):

24, 30 (all), 44, 74 (bl), 110, 114 (tc & tr), 128, 142, 148, 150, 162, 170, 172, 174, 180 (b), 184 (all), 196 (t & c), 198 (t & c), 210 (t & b), 212 (tr), 246, 260

PHOTOLIBRARY:

34: Oxford Scientific/Photolibrary

ISTOCKPHOTO:

© iStockphoto.com/Jimena Brescia: 42; © iStockphoto.com/Daniel Stein: 100 (tc); © iStockphoto.com/Anegada & Andrea Haase: 117; © iStockphoto.com/Jenny Speckels: 249; © iStockphoto.com/Stephan Messner: 255